Praise for *The Missing Manual to ___ ~, ~~~~riage and Intimacy:*

"Just reading the wisdom within these pages has already changed the way I approach all of my relationships. Tracie's golden guidance is spot on if you're attempting to repair or enhance your intimacy."

~Suzanne Mathis McQueen, author of *4 Seasons in 4 Weeks*

"Tracie Sage is a bundle of pure starlight and her book, *The Missing Manual to Love, Marriage and Intimacy*, is her wonderful gift to the world. It is an incredibly insightful yet playfully written handbook that will be useful to anyone whether you are currently in a relationship or not. Tracie's unwavering commitment to helping others and furthering the 'Love Evolution' movement shines through each and every page."

~Larry Korn, author of *One-Straw Revolutionary: The Philosophy and Work of Masanobu Fukuoka*

"As a Couple's Spiritual Intimacy Guide and woman of three former husbands, I am always excited to find new and engaging information to share with my clients (and myself!) Tracie Sage's toolbox of wisdom, gives the gift of choice to see the "glass half full" instead of half empty. Her reminder statements and clear questions give doable guidelines to the newly awakened. This is a perfect manual to relearn the path of compassionate relationship with a workbook edge. This book doesn't let you sit back and simply read. There's accountability. There's exercises. There's action steps. No guessing game here. Enjoy, apply, and celebrate the results!"

~Graell Corsini, author of *Mama Magick, Path of Sacred Living, and Goddess Sadhana*

Tracie Sage's clear wisdom sparkles on every page of this heart-centered yet practical manual. Applying the practices within this book, stirs our broken parts to heal, allowing us to participate more fully in our relationships and toward a more loving and peaceful world. Thank you, Tracie!

~ Deborah Perdue, author of *Daily Gratitude Reflections* and *Grace of Gratitude Journal*

The *Missing* MANUAL
to Love, Marriage and Intimacy

A Proactive Path
to Happily Ever After

TRACIE SAGE

The Missing Manual to Love, Marriage and Intimacy

Copyright © 2017 Tracie Sage

Published by
Applegate Valley Press

Edited by L. Lee Culvert

Book design by
Illumination Graphics

Author photo by Dave Levine

Softcover ISBN: # 978-0-9984916-0-8

In love, gratitude & celebration

of

Auntie Merle

Contents

$\mathcal{A}$cknowledgments

My Heartfelt Gratitude

This book was birthed in the extraordinary loving and nurturing embrace of Larry Morningstar, my dear, insightful, adoring avatar of love. I feel deeply grateful and blessed by your magical midwifery, your consistently generous spirit and your fun, charming, articulate reframes. You are precious to me. "I must have been Gandhi or Buddha or someone like that…"

My heartfelt gratitude and a huge hug of love to you, Mom. Thanks for being my greatest fan and steady encouragement throughout this journey. I cherish the qualities of our relationship and all the many hats we wear and ways we share our adventures of life together.

Special thanks to Dave Levine for giving my book your eagle-eye proofreading and giving me shelter from the storm during this last phase of writing. Thank you as well for your amazing ability to capture my essence through the eye of your camera. I feel seen in your photos. On top of that, I am repeatedly grateful for your comfy, cozy and Tracie-friendly guest room, your wit, charm and oh so many delicious meals and thoughtful ways. I love you dearly.

I am eternally grateful to Lee Culvert for being the outstanding editor you are. It has been a fun, educational and joyful process working with you. Thank you for your caring, brilliance and patience.

I'm sending an enormously loving thank-you to Christy Tryhus, my treasured coach, and to you, Deborah Perdue, my supremely talented, graphic designer angel. The beautiful being you are is reflected in your designs.

My heart is overflowing with love and gratitude for my dear ones who touch my life and my heart in so many rich and wonderful ways. Your immense support and understanding during this book journey made it possible. You are my village, enriching my life with abundant love and sweet moments shared.

I also want to honor and give thanks to my beloved angels, spirit guides and teachers, and to the leaders and forerunners of this love evolution—I am infinitely grateful.

Lastly, I am sending so much love and gratitude out to all my clients and students for sharing your courage and celebrations with me, for allowing me to do what I love and do best. I couldn't have written this book without you.

with love & hugs of gratitude, Tracie

Preface

I WAS BORN TO A SWEET, YOUNG NEWLYWED MOTHER who had just had her dream of happily ever after shattered to bits and pieces. Her marriage had gone from fun to fallen apart by the time she was six months pregnant. That was how I came into this lifetime . . . with a kinesthetic in utero preview of coming attractions.

As long as I can remember, I've always been fascinated by our human relationships and motivated by love. I have a very clear memory from when I was two years old witnessing my mother and my grandmother arguing and the pain they experienced in their relationship, knowing in my heart that there was a way to turn those arguments around to express the love underneath. I knew with all my senses that they loved each other as deeply as they hurt. I knew there was a better way. And . . . I knew it was for me to find out.

My child heart's desire for my Mom and grandmother to be happy together was a very strong motivation. From that moment on, I studied relationships intently, determined to help Mom and Nana heal their wounds and connect in a way that expressed the real love they had for each other. Over time, I saw that my mother and grandmother struggled in other relationships, too. They both had only unhappy marriages. My grandmother was married twice and gave up at the very young age of 54. Mom had three marriages before she called it quits at about that same age. I started taking mental notes of what worked and what failed to lead to the sweet closeness that I found so compelling.

My Nana told me that I began sharing little love wisdoms with her when I was five years old. Much later, she reminded me of some of my early words of wisdom that had stuck with her over the years. It was fun to hear and to recognize that those early insights had stuck with me too. They were the beginnings of love wisdom I've lived by and shared as the relationship mentor and role model for my friends, family, and eventually for my clients.

When I was nine, my mom married a man she had been dating, who had raised big red flags for me from the moment I met him. And although he became my physically, sexually and emotionally abusive stepfather, he could not damage my clear, courageous spirit. I remember walking on eggshells around him in fear of the pain and suffering he induced, yet still feeling empowered within my being. I felt held by a benevolent Universe and confident that my commitment to love, honesty and integrity would prevail. I moved out on my own when I was 15, and though I felt sad to leave my siblings and my mother, I also felt a great sense of freedom and possibility. I followed my heart's desire to start dancing, and discovered the healing power of expressive movement. Dancing was where my own healing journey began, which led me to movement therapy and then to yoga, loyal practices that continue to be a blessing in my life today. I learned to listen deeply and trust my body's messages as a way of receiving guidance.

I also stayed focused on and committed to learning what it takes to create the kind of loving relationships I knew were possible. I began exploring love and intimacy with my first Love when I was 14. Together we cultivated a mutually respectful, sweet, amazingly mature and supportive partnership, breaking the chain of dysfunctional, unhealthy relationships in my lineage fresh out of the gate. My relationships became the inspiration for friends and family, who came to me for guidance and support.

After years of being the go-to relationship support for the people around me, it was a natural progression for me to integrate all my healthy relationship tools and practices into my work as a movement therapist and teacher and ultimately as a love and relationship coach working with individuals and couples. By that time, I am delighted to say, Mom and Nana had indeed healed their relationship. They learned to see, hear and embrace each other in love, and enjoyed many years of fun times and sweet connection before my grandmother died.

In my own life, my informal yet astute relationship research from youth paid off. My inner chooser works well. With one exception, I've chosen to live, learn and explore in love with partners who were also committed to choosing connection and open, honest communication. We shared healthy, nourishing relationships with open, honest and loving transitions into friendship when our paths naturally parted ways. Our commitment to the quality of our connection and communication with each other created a safe and stable foundation for our growth and evolution as we navigated the issues and challenges that naturally arise in intimate relationships. Even when the form of our relationships changed, the love remained. In the one relationship I chose to explore without a mutual, conscious commitment to choosing connection and honesty, I gained a deeper understanding of unhealthy relationship dynamics and their impacts. I also earned the empathy I had lacked before about how compelling it can be to stay with an unhealthy relationship in hopes of reaching a turning point to healthy, happy rewards. All this to affirm that when the foundation remains unstable, no amount of loving repairs will prevent its collapse if we don't address the foundational problems. All the love we shared and all my relationship skills were not enough to compensate for the fractured foundation. I felt defeated. My spirit felt broken for the first time in my life. Through this relationship exploration, I learned first-hand how we can perpetuate the distance and keep love away even when, or *especially* when, we really long for the closeness of being fully embraced. On the positive side, many gems of wisdom in this manual might not have been included if I had not faced the challenges and discoveries I encountered on that personal growth journey. The contrast between that painful experience and the deeply nourishing rewards of being in healthy, conscious, deliciously adoring relationships has only enhanced my commitment and focus to share this possibility with as many people as I can.

My commitment is magnified by the fact that as a culture we have neglected to include love and relationship skills in our basic education. We also have very few role models of the kind of lasting love and intimacy I've experienced and choose to cultivate in my life.

I have written this book as the manual of love and relationship wisdom I wish each of us had as we were growing up. It includes the essence of what I've discovered so far about what works and what breaks us apart. I feel a passionate calling to reach as many people and touch as many lives as I can with this possibility of sweet, nourishing love and intimacy. My mission is to inspire a culture in which children grow up surrounded and embraced by healthy, loving relationship role models and, in turn, can create healthy, happy, loving relationships of their own.

May your relationships embrace and nourish you. May you adore and be deliciously adored, always.

In love,

Tracie

Introduction

How to receive the most from this book

Only one person has the power to change your life. Yes, YOU are the One.

You are also the only person who has the power to keep you from love or to choose love as a priority in your life. And YOU have the power to make that choice again, right now. By choosing to read this manual, you are taking a powerful step toward the love and intimacy you truly desire.

Most of what I am about to share with you, you already know . . . if not consciously, then instinctively. The trick is that knowing is not enough. You have to apply what you know and integrate it into your life and relationships in order for it to have the impact you desire.

If you really truly desire relationship miracles, you will only be able to create them when you actually integrate these relationship practices and apply the tools—just knowing about them will do very little if anything at all.

Ok then, are you ready to do something new, maybe even radically different, to have the love, intimacy and deeply nourishing relationship you are meant to share?

The key to using this book in a way that will help you create real love and intimacy, is to use it as a manual and to apply the tools and practices from each chapter into the moments of your daily life and relationships.

This manual is designed to give you the tools and practices that have worked again and again to help couples navigate the issues and challenges that naturally arise in intimate relationships. Implementing the tools in this manual will improve all your relationships and can be used whether you are married, in a partnership, or single. And though this book is written with heterosexual language for literary simplicity, most of these practices are equally applicable in gay and lesbian relationships as well.

Working through the manual together as a couple will exponentially enrich your assimilation process. However, it is not uncommon for one person in a couple to be ready and willing to make changes before the other. That's why my coaching is often done with individuals. This turns out to be very effective because as you begin using the tools, shifts and relationship miracles naturally occur pretty quickly. This positive response builds your confidence and reinforces your actions, while opening up a whole bunch of new possibilities, including that your partner may become curious about what's creating the positive shifts that are occurring, and may feel more motivated within your relationship. I have found that after I've been working with one person in a relationship for a few months, it is quite common for his or her partner to get on board for coaching as well, strengthening their commitment as a couple and accelerating their progress on the proactive path to love and intimacy.

Start by choosing one new practice or tool to explore and apply in your daily moments. Once you have assimilated the first practice, then you can add another one and so on. Follow your intuition to choose a practice that calls to you and seems likely to make a positive difference in your love life. Be sure to implement each practice fully, giving it your best effort along with an attitude of playful discovery and a sense of humor.

Allow yourself some time to cultivate and refine each new practice just as you might do if you were learning or deepening your experience of any new art or activity. Be patient with yourself as you expand your unique expression in this art of love. You probably still live in a culture of unhealthy relationships and have likely been practicing your old habits for most of your life, so it might take a little time of consistently practicing the new ones before they become completely yours. Studies show that for most of us, it takes six to ten months of training and consistent practice to integrate new relationship skills and responses into our daily lives. So, you've got to give it a good, honest test run to get real results.

Each chapter offers some structures and action steps you can use to support you in your journey and integration process. You'll find the following resources at the end of each chapter to help you:

Questions to ask:

Asking questions or being in a place of curiosity opens the door to discovering yourself, your partner, new solutions and new possibilities. It also invites the flow of insights and guidance. When you ask a question, you're letting the universe know what you're open to receiving or creating. So at the end of each chapter, I will give you questions to ask throughout your day. In order to keep the questions in your awareness, I encourage you to write them on sticky notes and place them where you're most likely to see them throughout the day (in your car, on the bathroom mirror, by your desk and your bed . . .). And every time you see the question, ask it out loud. Then stay open and alert to receiving direction, listening with all your senses. Guidance and insights may show up in many different forms. You may be guided to a book or a coach, a teacher or a resource. You may receive it in the form of thoughts. Or you may be guided by your feelings. Following feelings of fun and lightness usually lead the way toward fulfilled wishes. And sometimes you'll be blessed with an instant miracle. When you cultivate curiosity and keep asking questions, the doors of new possibilities stay open.

Tools and practices to use:

At the end of each chapter, as well as within the chapters, I will give you specific tools and practices to apply in your relationships and daily life. I'll be including guidance and details on how to integrate them. Choose one that resonates with you, as a starting point. Once you practice, explore and integrate that first one, then you might add another one and so on.

As I've indicated before, the principles in this manual only work if you take action by using the tools and practices that are included with each chapter. If you only store them as information or theory, they will do nothing to improve your relationship or to fulfill your desire for love and intimacy.

Actions to choose:

In this section, I will give you specific actions to take to integrate the key elements of the chapter into your relationship and your life. Choose an action that is in alignment with your desires for your relationship. Commit to the action by scheduling it in your calendar.

Celebrations!

Celebrate *every* time you make a shift, have a new awareness or insight, make a new choice, take an action in alignment with what you desire or experience a miracle! Celebrations can be as simple as pausing to acknowledge a shift with a deep breath and a smile, a dance of joy, a hoot and a holler, sharing your success with your coach or a loved one, or anything else that feels fun and acknowledges the shifts and miracles taking place, whether huge or small.

Further notes before you begin . . .

Don't take my word for it!

Personally, I don't take anything as true for me until I explore what's possible by applying, in my own life, whatever sounds too good to be true that I would actually love to be true. This keeps my points of view and limiting beliefs from getting in the way of living my dreams. The worst case scenario is I'm still where I started and nothing shifted. Often, I discover what is truly possible even beyond my own visions and dreams. How does it get any better than that?

So, don't just believe what is written in this manual. Though you may resonate with much of it, and feel or know it to be true for you, you may still find yourself holding onto the old habits, patterns and relationships that don't work. This is most likely because it is more comfortable and less scary than making changes that are radically different from what you've been doing. You will have the most potent and irreversible results when you give this a full test run in your own life! This is the only way to know what will actually create lasting love and relationship miracles for you!

The other thing to remember is that many or most of the relationships and people surrounding you are not likely to be practicing much of what's in this manual. In fact, some of the guidelines are radically opposed to what we're used to and surrounded by in our culture. So it may be best to approach this as a grand experiment. Create the "experiment" conditions that will truly support your new practices and the impact you wish to create in your love life. Surround yourself with people who support you and create structures for yourself that support you to integrate these changes into your life. My love and blessings are with you every step of the way.

1

What Ever Happened to Happily Ever After?

Where did we go astray?

Have you been feeling disappointed, lonely or rejected in love?

Do you long for more intimacy, cuddles and closeness?

Are you frequently frustrated and annoyed with your partner? Do you live with tension between you?

Or, are you single and settling, having completely given up on the possibility of the kind of love you've always dreamed of sharing with that special someone?

If you answered yes to any of these questions, the first secret I want to share with you is that you are not alone! And you are not to blame!

Right now, we are facing an epidemic of lonely people and unhappy break-ups, leaving a wake of broken families and a multitude of discouraged singles. Our divorce rate and the number of people over age forty who have not yet been married are both higher than ever. As a culture, we seem to under-value the importance of our intimate connections or the nourishment of feeling loved and adored.

We distract ourselves in countless unfulfilling ways and even act as if our social needs can be met via cyber connection. It certainly seems simpler and safer to have remote relationships when we don't really know *how* to cultivate nourishing intimate ones. And, without much guidance on how to navigate the issues and challenges that naturally arise in our intimate relationships, chances are we've had some discouraging experiences and heartbreaks without having a clear view of how to do it any differently. Even people who go out and socialize frequently, often tell me they feel sad, lonely and isolated because they're still missing and longing for the deeply nourishing embrace of real love and closeness.

As a love and relationship coach, I hear the personal stories, see the wounds and witness the impact of dysfunction, both up-close and in the bigger picture. Do you ever wonder why both depression and addictions have become so normal and commonplace? Could loneliness and heartache have something to do with it?

How important is love, really?

What does love do for you?

Why is love the topic of so many movies, TV shows, books, songs, blogs and magazine articles? What difference does love make?

The importance of our intimate connections cannot be underestimated . . .

Studies have shown that close, loving relationships are essential to our wellbeing and happiness. Based on my experience as a love coach and as a human being, I wholeheartedly agree. The benefits of sharing healthy, loving, intimate relationships are rich and rewarding.

Here are some common benefits derived from healthy love and intimacy:

~ Shared connection and understanding, inspiration and encouragement

~ Physical touch, pleasure and nurturing

~ Being and feeling seen, embraced and supported

~ The joys of giving and receiving

~ Companionship and collaboration for the fun and challenging adventures of life

~ Safety, security and support to grow and evolve . . . becoming our best selves

Looking at this list, we can easily see why we long to have a truly loving, intimate connection and what an immense contribution it can be to our health, happiness, success and thriving. The truth is, we know inherently that love is good for us.

How much more love and intimacy would you like to invite into *your* life?

What would it take for you to let in enough love to thrive?

Love is also healing. Good relationships with friends, family and partners not only make us feel better, research has shown that these relationships actually have a physical effect that helps to prevent illness and helps us recover from illness more quickly. Loving touch, for example, is being used in many ways—from pediatric care to care of older adults—to promote healing. How healthy would we be if we made it a priority to get our daily dose of love and physical touch?

The emotional exchange that takes place whenever someone touches us lovingly, or when we do the same for someone else, increases blood flow and deeply nourishes the heart. As the center of our physical being, the heart receives loving touch as a message, translated instantly into a powerful bio-chemical response.

Imagine the benefits of living in this love . . . feeling loved and adored, our hearts being touched frequently in meaningful ways and stimulating our feel-good hormones. Clearly, the impor-tance of our intimate connections cannot be underestimated, and feeling loved and adored may be as beneficial to our health as a balanced diet and exercise.

So . . . whatever happened to happily ever after and where did we go astray?

Well, let's be curious about this together.

Think of all the couples you know who seem to have the keys to thriving together in love or the heart-warming stories you've heard about someone's parents or grandparents who shared a healthy, loving relationship. If you search for these stories back through generations, do you find them to be the exception or the rule? We often idealize our past. What if it's just a romantic myth that, at one time in human history, "happily ever after" was the prevailing paradigm? Could it be similar to our vision of a peaceful world without war, which has not yet been realized? How can we create peace in the world until we are able to create connected, loving relationships with our dear ones, our families, our neighbors and our communities?

It has been documented that more people got married and stayed married prior to the mid-20th century, yet there is little evidence to show that those marriages were predominantly happy or healthy. It seems that financial dependency was the glue that kept plenty of couples married in the past, and not necessarily the joys of sharing a life together. Since we no longer view marriage as a necessary means of survival, single parenting has been on the rise, and now up to 40% of all children are reported to be born outside of marriage.

The impact of this trend may be more devastating than we even recognize. In the recent book by William Tucker, "Marriage and Civilization: How Monogamy Made Us Human," we learn that a leading indicator of whether someone will be inclined toward poverty or know prosperity is whether, while growing up, he or she knew the love and security of having a married mother and father. Tucker also notes that, based on the work of Charles Murray, the art of fatherhood does not come naturally but is a skill that must be passed on from generation to generation. What if the keys

Happily ever after doesn't just happen because you've found the love of your life. Happiness is a personal choice.

to healthy, happy relationships must also be passed forward from generation to generation?

What if children grew up with parents who modeled a loving relationship, who openly showed each other affection and respect, expressing feelings authentically, and who lovingly, even playfully, turned conflicts toward solutions. What if we grew up feeling embraced, loved, seen and valued for the whole of who we are? Would it all turn out differently? You bet it would!

Where does this leave us now?

When was the last time you witnessed a real, live relationship that had the qualities of happily ever after? Not the Hollywood or fantasy kind, where conditions are idyllic or unnatural, but the real-life kind. Have you witnessed relationships in which the commitment to real understanding, honesty and love created ease even in difficult situations? Did you notice that palpable quality of joy, depth and ease in their intimate connection? Have you seen how the foundation of caring and kindness with each other framed their human mistakes, failures and growth in a beautiful, embracing way? These are characteristics of real-life examples of the kind of loving relationships that are possible for all of us. Yet they seem to be the rare exceptions to the rule. Most of our parents didn't model or even know how to create such a deeply nourishing, harmonious marriage, and in many cases, neither did our grandparents nor our great-grandparents.

For most of us, the role models we have of happy, healthy, thriving marriages are few to none. Think about it! How many couples do you know who have been together for more than a few years, who have the kind of loving relationship and intimate connection you would really want?

Starting in childhood, we have successful role models, teachers and mentors built into our lives for just about anything else we choose to succeed in. However, for most of us, when it comes to love, intimacy and marriage, we just don't know many people who really do the relationship thing much better than we do. So, without role models, mentors, education or a manual for how to have healthy, happy, loving relationships, let alone intimacy and marriage, how can we expect ourselves to know how to develop the deeply nourishing love and intimacy we truly desire?

The good news is that you are holding the manual that has been missing until now.

Contrary to many of our fairy tales and movies, "happily ever after" doesn't just happen because you've found the love of your life. Happiness is a personal choice. No one can give you happily ever after unless you are choosing it. What if happily ever after is a path you can choose and not "The End"?

This book will take you beyond where most fairy tales and movies end. In your day-to-day, moment-by-moment adventures of life, you and your Love *can* actually create your very own happily ever after together. This is possible when you are both *proactively* choosing happiness and prioritizing your relationship. We are programmed to associate happily ever after with the end of the story, rather than the quality of the journey. Sharing the journey can make it richer, sweeter and in some ways easier. And, it is all much more likely if you embrace the whole adventure, including the many opportunities for growth that arise along the way.

Happily ever after doesn't just happen. Love is a practice. It's up to you to choose it, prioritize it and commit to it.

What about the bigger picture?

Since the late 1980s, we've had some glimpses and break-throughs, visionaries and leaders in our love evolution. And we are currently in a time of accelerated human awakening. You may have heard the saying that the darkest hour is just before the dawn. We've seen this pattern in our history again and again, where in the midst of one paradigm crumbling and magnifying our suffering, the next wave of visionaries is rising and spreading new solutions that catalyze our evolution. The time is Now! Since you are reading this, I know you are responding to the calling to participate in this love evolution movement and together we are surfing this wave to a new paradigm of happily ever after.

Let's do this for ourselves! Let's do it for our children!

Congratulations!

You have just taken a courageous step toward expanding your capacity to love and be loved and to having the intimate relationship you truly desire. This manual will give you essential relationship practices and tools you didn't receive growing up. As you integrate these practices and tools into your relationships and your love life, you will open the door to creating the kind of love and intimacy you long to have and that we all need in order to be truly healthy, happy people. And you do not have to do this all on your own. In fact, the more support you gather around you, the more ease, fun and impact your love journey will have. So . . . here goes!

Love is a practice. It's up to you to choose it, prioritize it and commit to it.

As you read this manual, absorbing its message of new possibilities and as you start integrating the love practices and tools in your relationships, I invite you to share your journey and inspiration with your friends and loved ones. Create a supportive environment for your new choices, growth and evolution in love. Surround yourself with others who are willing to join you in discovering the common habits that consistently lead to disappointments in love and who are ready to learn and apply the key practices to turn them around. Cultivate connections with inspirational couples, relationship mentors and happy, healthy role models in your life. Give yourself the advantage of all the support you need to shift those limiting beliefs and unhealthy patterns acquired through culture and family and years of exposure to unhealthy and dysfunctional relationship role models.

Now that you have followed your heart to a place where you have access to love wisdom and mentoring, you are on a proactive path to your very own happily ever after.

Welcome to the rich and rewarding journey of discovering what else is possible in love, marriage and intimacy!

Questions to ask:

Asking questions opens you to new possibilities and solutions. No need to know or find the answers. Just ask the question with a sense of curiosity, speaking out loud if possible, and then release it. Be open to new insights and possibilities. Stay tuned to what shows up. Guidance may come instantly or later. It may come as new awareness, feelings, thoughts, images, or in other forms. Asking opens the door to miracles.

What choice can I make in this moment to nourish my own happiness?

What else is possible if I choose love right now?

What would love do?

What is the most loving choice I can make here?

What action or step can I take to move towards the love, happiness and amazing relationship I am meant to share?

How much more fun can we have together if we begin proactively choosing and committing to happily ever after as our path?

What if we become the ones who live and model conscious, loving relationships?

What difference would that make to our children, our community and future generations?

Tools and practices to use:

1) Choosing Love Practice:

Choose love. Choose happiness. Choose again. Each moment of your life, every interaction, is an opportunity to choose. You can choose consciously or unconsciously. Practice choosing consciously.

Actions to choose:

This is simply a list of actions based on this chapter that you might choose to take on your proactive path. I offer them as options to support you in bringing the material from this manual to life. You may choose one or more from this list or you may find something else from the chapter that inspires your action. The practices work miracles when practiced! And to enjoy the shifts and miracles, you'll need to take actions!

Action1: Choose another chapter that calls to you. Read it and choose one new practice or tool to integrate into your daily life and relationships. You can practice with your partner or a friend or family member, or even a co-worker or . . . Most of the practices can be applied in all your relationships to navigate issues and challenges and to enhance connection, understanding, fun and harmony.

Action 2: Make a list of encouraging couples, friends and people you know who see, embrace and support all of who you are. Keep that list handy as a reminder of where you might experiment with your new practices and tools or to whom you might reach out for support and encouragement.

Action 3: Cultivate connections with inspirational couples, relationship mentors and happy, healthy role models in your life. Surrounding yourself and infusing your daily life with inspiring influences is the quickest and most effective way to make changes.

continued...

Actions to choose:

continued

Action 4: Think of one friend with whom you'd love to share your discoveries on your path to more love and intimacy. You might invite your partner and/or your friend to read the book with you too.

Action 5: Read the "Introduction: How to receive the most from this book."

Celebrations!

Celebrate *every* time you make a shift, have a new awareness or insight, make a new choice, take an action in alignment with what you desire or experience a miracle! Celebrations can be as simple as pausing to acknowledge a shift with a deep breath and a smile, a leap of joy, a hoot and a holler, sharing your success with your coach or a loved one, or anything else that feels fun and acknowledges the shifts and miracles taking place, whether small or huge.

2

The Four Keys to the Gates of Love

*Four Relationship Secrets You Need to Know
to Keep the Magic Alive*

THE FOUR KEYS TO THE GATES OF LOVE INTRODUCED in this chapter will give you access to the deeply nourishing love and intimate relationship you are meant to share. They will also help you to cultivate the safety and security you need to resolve issues that naturally arise in your intimate connections. Using these keys you'll build a foundation of love, trust and fun, essential elements for creating a healthy, thriving relationship.

These four keys come directly from my work with individuals and couples, as well as my own personal experience in creating healthy, nourishing relationships. I like to call these love secrets the "AC/DC of Relationship"—the four key practices that keep the currents of love, trust, and fun flowing in our intimate connections. AC stands for Authentic Appreciation and Courageous Communication. I think of these two practices as the alternating current that allows our relationship to travel the distance without losing energy. In other words it keeps the relationship juicy! DC stands for Deep Listening and Commitment, which together generate the direct current that gives our relationship stability. Let me illuminate how you can apply these four keys to keep the current flowing in your relationships.

The Four Keys to the Gates of Love

Key #1: Authentic Appreciation

Appreciation goes a long way to feed our love. When we express our authentic appreciations and gratitude sincerely, specifically and frequently, we feel more connection and aliveness in our relationship.

Imagine how you would feel as your Love sincerely expresses to you how much she appreciates you and is seeing how fabulous you really are. Do you feel closer to her? Notice how your body feels when you imagine receiving her authentic appreciation. And how inspired do you feel now to give her more of what you know she appreciates?

Your partner who loves you wants to please you, though he may not always know how. So appreciation lets him know when he's on the right track. It is a very loving way to inspire more of what you want. However, what often occurs after the honeymoon is over, and sometimes even sooner, is that we start to focus on what we *don't* want or what *doesn't* work, instead of what we appreciate. I've seen that giving attention to what's missing rapidly creates distance, frustration and discouragement and builds tension in the relationship, while appreciation can prevent or reverse it!

Put authentic appreciation to work in your relationship for some sweet surprises.

How do you feel when someone tells you something like: "It really bothers me when you talk to me like that"? My initial response would be to shut down or run away, even though I know it would bring us closer if, instead, I could be curious and respond by asking: "What would feel better to you? How do you want me to talk to you"? However, when we're feeling hurt, we may not always choose the highest or most direct path to what we really desire.

So here's where we can make it easier for each other. If, when I spoke to my partner in a way that pleased him, he responded by saying, "When you look me in the eyes and talk to me softly and directly, as you just did, my heart opens and I want to listen to what you are saying to me." Now I feel good and I'm going to remember that feedback. He also made it easy for me to do it again because he was specific about the qualities that pleased him: "looking him in the eyes," "speaking softly and directly." So, he has inspired me with appreciation rather than pushing me away with dissatisfaction.

Now it's your turn. Put this key of authentic appreciation to work in your relationship for some sweet surprises,

Make a commitment to authentically reveal yourself, sharing your whole self.

including more of what you love. Be sure to speak honestly and sincerely. The easiest way to do this is to notice and appreciate the things that warm your heart or touch you in a positive way. And it may be awkward at first. With practice, it will eventually become easy and natural.

Key #2: Courageous Communication

It takes courage to show up fully, to be fully present and honest, owning our feelings and expressing our truth with our partner. Sometimes it even takes courage to simply feel our feelings. At first, I had named this secret "Communication" and then realized that, more than just communicating, it's the quality and intention of our communication with one we love that is the true key.

The qualities that allow us to connect in a meaningful way include being present, authentic and honest. Being present means connecting to your breath, your body and your feelings. You may be wondering: "How do I do that"? The first step is to make the choice to be present, and then take a few deep breaths while giving your attention to how you feel. This simple effort to get connected usually takes only a few seconds once you choose to do so. By giving yourself your own attention first, you will become more available to connect with your partner as well.

I find that yoga offers a great way to practice becoming present and connected with our own feelings and truth, as well as helping us to tap into our own source of courage. This is why I often combine yoga and coaching on my retreats, and also when I work with couples who are willing to include yoga in their program along with love coaching.

Another way to deepen connection and build trust with one you love is by making a commitment to authentically reveal yourself. Revealing yourself means sharing your whole self, including your vulnerabilities, feelings and concerns, as well as being honest about the parts of you that you don't completely love and embrace.

When you choose to get in touch with your own feelings and desires, own them as yours, and take full responsibility for them, you'll profoundly increase the levels of fun, trust and closeness you share in your relationship.

Another aspect of courageous communication is asking your Love for support by making clear, specific, and do-able requests. This allows your Love to know what you really want and to support and love you in the way you want to be loved. It takes away the burden of having to figure it out and allows your partner to support you more easily.

An important part of making a request is being willing to accept a "no." If you are not allowing room for the "no," you are making a demand, and most of us do not respond well to demands because they take away our sense of freedom. When we infringe upon another person's freedom, it often meets with resistance and will likely push them away from us even if they comply, rather than creating the closeness we really want. So, when you are making a request, check in with yourself and if you are not ready to accept a "no," look within to find the fear beneath your need to control the situation. Once you have this awareness, you can authentically reveal your inner challenge with your partner, instead of making a demand.

I find that courageous communication is the most challenging secret for me to apply consistently. It can be quite scary to speak my truth in moments when I'm not feeling safe or secure. These moments offer me an opportunity to own and reveal my fear. When I gather my courage to share my vulnerability and express what's true for me, I am often rewarded with feelings of relief, freedom and greater closeness. It reminds me of diving into a cold river. I love swimming in rivers for the nourishment it gives me and I go almost every week during the warm season. Yet, I still have to rally my courage each time I dive in even though I know from experience that I'll feel exhilarated when I do. I also notice that when I practice my courageous communication often, I get into the flow and when I get out of practice I find it much harder to dive in again.

As with most things, the more we practice, the easier it becomes! And it gets much easier as we build trust and safety in our relationship using these next two secrets.

Key #3: Deep Listening

"Deep listening" is listening with all your senses to what wants to be heard and felt. This is the flip side of Key #2. The more inviting, allowing and embracing you are with your loved one, the safer it is for them to reveal and share themselves with you. Be curious about yourself and your Love. Be willing to hold space for your Love to show up authentically with feelings, vulnerabilities and desires of his/her own. Be curious. Ask for clarification and check out your understanding.

Listening is one of the sweetest ways of enhancing your connection by building safety and trust that draws you closer together. For many people this is also extremely attractive and can be an often overlooked, yet exceptionally powerful, aphrodisiac. Don't take my word for it though. Try it and see for yourself! And do let me know if you get any surprising results that please you.

Key #4: Commitment

When you commit to your connection and to creating the relationship you truly desire, results will show up as tangible and powerful energetic shifts. If we want different results, we have to make new choices and take different actions.

An effective commitment begins with a conscious choice. You need to choose and commit to what you truly want in your relationship. If you want intimacy, you have to choose and commit to being intimate. If you want kindness and honesty in your relationship, you have to commit to being kind and honest. If you want to unstick your relationship, you have to commit to clearing anything that keeps you stuck and choose to do what it takes. It's especially powerful to write and speak your commitments out loud, even more so when witnessed. This is the inspiration for the wedding ceremony in which a couple speaks their commitments witnessed by the friends, family and community that will support their journey together. Commitment inspires natural shifts and new levels of clarity and honesty, making it a great way to revive a stagnant relationship or begin a new one.

Just like anything else you desire to have or create in life, your results reflect your investment of energy in the forms of time, attention and money. Time: Give some time to connecting in all the ways I mentioned in the first three keys. Give yourself and your relationship time for fun. Attention: Allow yourself to be more aware of your part in your relationship. The first step in creating change is awareness. Ask your Love what would keep the relationship fun and fulfilling for him/her. Ask for clear, specific, doable requests. Follow through on any agreements you make. Money: Invest in things that support your relationship. This might include vacations, retreats or other activities you enjoy together, relationship support, coaching and mentoring, books, recordings and more. Put your energy, time, attention and money toward your dreams and desires.

Be willing to go through the growth challenges as well as the comfortable phases. Allow for new learning, growth, change and evolution. Change is a natural part of our lives. Without the natural flow of growth and evolution, both relationships and people die.

How the four keys work in real life.

Here's a true story of how the keys I've just shared with you work when you put them into practice. A couple, Gabe and Jill, came to me as a last-ditch effort when they were at the point of breaking up. It is very common for couples to wait until it's too late before getting help, and this was the most dramatic expression of that I've ever seen. Their body language was profound!

The couple walked into the room and sat as far away from each other as they could, facing away from each other. And I thought, "Oh my goodness, I can't even believe these two made it into this room." Since they had made it, I trusted that there was some little ember of possibility worth fanning so I worked with them, and even within that first session, I started noticing shifts. Jill was ready for the help and she was steaming angry, so once we established a level of safety and connection, I was able to give her some healthy ways to move through her anger and to offer Gabe a safe way to support her. First, we had to get clear on what they were there to do and be sure that they were both on board for moving forward. During this initial process, Gabe, who I could tell had a lot of resistance, told me, "I really wasn't going to come, she was just out the door and there was no other way . . . this was the only thing I could do." He also realized early on in the session that he was in a safe place and that the coaching was actually *helpful. He even acknowledged this when I encouraged him to speak his truth about something he was holding back and needed to own, which allowed him to drop into really feeling himself, and to being honest in that moment, in a way that completely honored and acknowledged him. Speaking our truth and taking responsibility for our own choices and actions is incredibly liberating and can be both healing and empowering in our relationships. We often avoid owning our part, fearing that we'll feel guilty when the truth is that our guilt and fear are already dominating the situation, wreaking havoc in our relationship and on how we feel about ourselves, which only widens the gap between us. Gabe was showing up! By the end of the session, they were both open to doing more work and ready to take some new practices home with them.*

The next session was about a week later. They came in and sat two feet away from each other and facing toward each other now. No, not even two feet, they were a foot apart because they were able to touch each other. And what they told me was, "This is amazing. You brought the fun back into our relationship. It's been gone for years." It was *amazing! And I didn't do it. I just gave them the keys. Only they could use them to unlock the gates of love that had been closed up in their relationship. It was truly a love miracle. This is why I do what I do and feel so strongly called to write this book to share what is truly possible. And ... it takes commitment as well as devoted practice to access love miracles and keep those embers alive.*

Now, I have to tell you the sad truth beyond the encouraging portion of this story, which is that they stopped coming for coaching after that. They felt so good and so confident after that second session that they didn't continue working with me. They did the other most common thing that sabotages many loving relationships, which is they didn't stay with the relationship support and love mentoring they needed for as long as it takes to replace old unhealthy habits with new nourishing practices until they are completely integrated. About three months later Jill and Gabe called me in crisis because they were splitting up in a painfully disconnected way. My heart went out to them. Imagine if they had come to me sooner and had chosen to stay with it . . .

The gift in all this was that I got to see how effective and powerful these tools and practices truly are. Even a couple so far out the door could have a turn around. It also inspired me to create a new way of working with couples that allows for more immediate integration and long-term progress with built-in extended support. So, the moral of this story, which I am highlighting so that you will take note, is this: Don't wait to get help *while the gap of distance and destruction is growing wider between you and the one you love.* And do stay with it, *gathering all the support and mentoring you need until you've fully integrated enough nourishing practices and tools to sustain and expand the love and intimacy that's truly possible in your relationship.*

Opening the Gates of Love

Now that you know the Four Keys to open the Gates of Love, you can establish and renew the foundation of love, trust and fun in your relationship. If you are ready to start getting results that will please you, your next step will be to put these secrets into practice in your relationship on a moment-to-moment and daily basis.

Start by using just one key and opening one gate at a time. Be patient with yourself and stay with it. When you feel ready, then open a second gate. Eventually you can open all four gates, integrating all the secrets in your day-to-day moments and interactions. Many couples get immediate results and sometimes they have to practice for a bit to experience the benefits.

As always, don't take my word for any of this. Give it the full test for a good six months or longer and see for yourself!

Remember, the tools can only work miracles if you practice them. The more consistently you practice, the more you'll enjoy consistent and pleasing results. My intention is to inspire you to implement these practices and tools into your everyday moments so you can enjoy deeply nourishing love and intimacy, celebrating the kinds of love miracles I've seen again and again.

Questions to ask:

Asking questions opens us to new possibilities and solutions. No need to know or find the answers. Just ask the question with a sense of curiosity, speaking out loud if possible, and then release it. Be open to new insights and possibilities. Stay tuned to what shows up. Guidance may come instantly or later. It may come as new awareness, feelings, thoughts, images, or in other forms. Asking opens the door to miracles.

What choice can I make in this moment to nourish my relationship?

What do I love most about my partner? How does that show up?

How can I be even more open and honest in revealing myself to dear ones?

How can I be even more open and honest in revealing myself to my Love?

How can I be more authentic right now?

How can I embrace all of my feelings and desires?

How can I recognize the guidance and messages my feelings give to me?

What can I do or shift to be an even better listener?

What commitments can I make now to honor the relationship I desire and choose to create? How can I be even more committed to my own happiness?

Tools and practices to use:

1) Authentic Appreciation Practice:

Notice the things people do that warm your heart or touch you in positive ways. Notice how you feel in your body (tingly, warm and fuzzy, energized . . .) and how you feel emotionally (happy, delighted, joyful, excited, motivated . . .) Begin speaking what you notice as authentic appreciations, shared with those people. Here's a simple formula to follow if this is new or awkward for you: I felt (describe what you felt physically and/or emotionally), when you (describe specifically what they did or said that touched you). You can begin with "Thank you for . . ." or "I appreciate you for . . ." or " I appreciated that you . . ." or "I feel blessed by . . ." Expressing authentic appreciation becomes easier with practice and will bring rich rewards to you and your relationships, so keep practicing!

continued...

Tools and practices to use continued

2) Courageous Communication Practice:
Begin by connecting with yourself. Take a few deep breaths and notice how you feel physically, emotionally and energetically. Check in and notice what's true for you in this moment. Ask yourself if there's something you are wanting right now. If so, acknowledge it to yourself. Practice noticing and then sharing what you notice with your partner. Is there anything you're hiding or withholding from your partner? If you feel afraid to share, that's a good place to begin. You can simply say, "I feel scared to tell you . . . I'm afraid (name what your fear is)."

Sometimes it helps to have a list of feelings to help identify and put into words exactly what you are feeling. You can find one online compiled by the Center for Nonviolent Communication. This list can also help make the distinction between feelings and thoughts, which are not usually as valuable for creating connection and can even get in the way of closeness. Learning what thoughts to share and how to share them in a way that deepens connection and builds trust is a more advanced practice so start with your physical and emotional feelings. Next, you can practice sharing your desires and making clear requests.

3) Deep Listening Practice:
Practice listening with all your senses. Listen deeply, beyond the words. Practice listening without reacting, interrupting or taking anything personally. Remember to breathe as you listen. Cultivate an attitude of curiosity. Ask about feelings or desires to invite deeper connection like an archeologist digging to unearth the treasures. Ask questions rather than assuming you understand. You'll learn more about the unique ways your partner experiences the world that way. And your partner will experience the sweet gift of feeling heard. As you listen to your partner, do your best to stay connected with yourself too.

4) Yoga and/or Meditation Practice:
Practice Yoga and/or meditation on a daily basis. Even twenty minutes each day will make a profound difference in how you show up in your relationships with yourself and others. I have found yoga and meditation to be the most helpful foundational relationship practices to support the essential skills of being a witness to yourself and others. They strengthen the core muscles needed in both Courageous Communication and Deep Listening, offering a great way to practice becoming present and connected with our own feelings and truth, as well as helping us to tap into our own source of courage. Through cultivating focused awareness, we are better able to receive messages from our inner guidance as well as the verbal and nonverbal messages of other beings. Yoga is the practice of cultivating awareness with breath and loving kindness. Meditation is the practice of focusing the mind. Combining them brings a profound state of calm aliveness and presence.

continued...

Tools and practices to use continued

5) Choosing Your Core Commitments Tool:

Core commitments are in alignment with your dreams and desires. In this case we will focus specifically on your relationship dreams and desires. You can also use this tool to create commitments in support of other dreams and desires. First make a list of essential qualities or changes you want in your relationship. Now prioritize the list by assigning a number to each quality or change. Starting with your number one priority, what new commitment do you need to make in order to cultivate that quality in yourself? Remember, you need to commit to choosing whatever it is you want in your relationship. So in the moments of choice that arise throughout each day, you'll have the chance to choose to honor your commitment again and again. Write your commitment and then speak it out loud with sincerity. To give it even more power, invite your partner or a friend to witness you as you speak your commitment. Here's an example of this process: Let's say you want to end the power struggle dynamic in your relationship. You can commit to choose love instead of clinging to being right when the power struggles arise. You write your commitment in the present and affirmative. "I commit to choosing love and letting go of needing to be right, especially when I catch myself in a power dynamic with (insert your partner's name here)." Follow voicing your commitment with acting on it in your moment-to-moment interactions. If and when you fall back into your old behaviors, be gentle with yourself. Remember that the old behavior is something you've practiced more than the new one you are now choosing. So, notice that you've fallen into a default pattern that no longer serves you, then forgive yourself and recommit to the new way you are choosing to be and act now. It is natural to veer off our chosen path every now and then, especially when we are in the process of developing a new course. Commitment is this process of coming back to the path you are choosing again and again.

6) Priority Assessment Tool:
Here's a great way to take an honest look at what you are currently prioritizing. This will let you see the position your relationship currently holds in your stack of priorities. Do be completely honest with yourself. And don't use this assessment to judge yourself as right or wrong or any other way. Instead just be curious to discover where and how you can make any shifts needed to raise your relationship to the level of priority you now choose. This Priority Assessment Tool can be used to evaluate other aspects of your life as well.

Step 1: Spatial Priority Assessment
Walk around your home and make a list in the order of most to least (percentages optional) of what fills the space of your home's real estate. How much of your home is devoted to connecting with each other or things that nourish you and your relationship? How much do you actually utilize these areas? What takes up the most of your space? How might these priorities be keeping you from the relationship you truly desire?

continued...

Tools and practices to use <small>continued</small>

Example list:

Love, connection, yoga, meditation & rest areas 34%

Cooking and eating areas 20%

Desk, files and computer 11%,

Clothing, shoes and accessories 8%

Bath and beauty 8%

Woodstove and supplies 7%

Books and reading areas 6%

Plants 3%

Other 3%

Step 2: Money Priority Assessment

Now take a look at your bookkeeping records and make a list starting with highest expense to lowest. Then review the list seeing the highest to lowest expenses as your highest to lowest priority. Now pull out the amount of money you spent on things that truly nourished your relationship. Look at where this amount falls in your list of priorities. What new awareness did this review give you?

Step 3: Time Priority Assessment

Make a list of the things you do each day with the amount of hours you do each of them. Now rewrite the list from highest number of hours to lowest. Where does your connection and relationship nourishment fall on this list? What did you discover?

Actions to choose:

This is simply a list of actions based on this chapter that you might choose to take on your proactive path. I offer them as options to support you in bringing the material from this manual to life. You may choose one or more from this list or you may find something else from the chapter that inspires your action. The practices work miracles when practiced! And to enjoy the shifts and miracles, you'll need to take actions!

Action 1: Choose a tool or practice from this chapter to apply in your daily life. Choose one that resonates with you, as a starting point. Once you practice, explore and integrate that first one, then you might add another one and so on.

continued...

Actions to Choose continued

Action 2: Begin creating your own collection of practice cards by writing each practice or tool that you wish to apply in your daily life on its own index card. Include all the specific steps or guidelines so you have everything you need on your card and you won't have to go searching for details later. The idea behind this action is to make these tools as handy as possible so it's easy to use and benefit from them. Writing each one out by hand helps you integrate the practice through your mind body connection and allows it to become your own. I invite you to get as colorful and creative with your cards as you like. Allowing this journey to be creative and fun engages both sides of your brain in the process for even better integration. This card system works best when you create a specific location or "home" where you keep them so you can always find them. You may also want to create a special container for your cards (a box, envelope, basket or something else that is accessible and sacred) as a way of highlighting or honoring the important role that your new practices play in your shift toward greater connection and intimacy. Over time your collection of tools and practices will grow and you'll have them all easily accessible whenever you need them as valuable resources. You can flip through your cards and choose one any time you need the support of a new practice or reminders to help you make the most of the practices you are choosing.

Action 3: Start or renew your yoga and/or meditation practice. To get yourself off to an easier start, you might want to attend a series of classes or receive some private yoga sessions. My favorite way to establish or renew a steady personal practice is to immerse myself on a retreat. You might choose a retreat close to home or if you enjoy traveling you could choose a retreat that takes place in a destination of interest to you. Your retreat could be just a weekend retreat or one that lasts a week or more. Choose whatever feels most fun and inspiring for you.

Action 4: Use the Priority Assessment Tool from the previous section to assess where your relationship currently falls in your list of priorities. What did you learn from the three-step assessment process? Did your honest assessment reveal anything that is keeping you from giving your relationship the attention it needs to be as amazing as you want it to be? What could you shift to raise your relationship to the level of priority you now choose?

Bonus action: Write to me with your love miracles and I will celebrate each and every one! You will also be contributing to our love evolution movement by creating an expanding culture of healthy, thriving relationships in the world. I am exhilarated and motivated by your love miracle stories and the extraordinary results that unfold when you implement these simple yet powerful practices into your life.

continued...

Celebrations!

Celebrate every time you make a shift, have a new awareness or insight, make a new choice, take an action in
alignment with what you desire or experience a miracle.
Celebrations can be as simple as pausing to acknowledge
a shift with a deep breath and a smile, a dance of joy, a
hoot and a holler, sharing your success with a loved one
or anything else that feels fun and acknowledges the shifts
and miracles taking place, whether small or huge.

3

The Most Common Destructive Habits in Relationships

And How to Turn Them Around

IN THIS CHAPTER, WE'LL LOOK AT THE HABITS and patterns that most frequently create distance and disconnection in relationships. Over time, these habits and patterns may lead to wounded hearts and broken relationships by destroying the love, trust and fun that once nourished closeness and intimacy. I'll also share the key practices you can use to turn each of these patterns of destruction around.

The first step is to become aware of each habit so that you can recognize when you're in it. As you start to recognize the habit, you'll be able to choose the key practice that will help you shift from pushing your partner away to inviting more love, understanding and kindness into your interactions. Each moment of recognition is worth celebrating even if it doesn't happen until after the fact. After a while, you'll be able to catch the pattern in the moment and make a new choice, then and there. With practice, you'll be able to eliminate the encounters altogether by establishing completely new ways of responding to situations as they arise. Every step of the way, you'll be cultivating a much more allowing, generously kind and caring point of view.

How much more connection and closeness can you cultivate with new awareness and key practices? How much suffering will you soothe? How much love will you uncover?

Are you willing to find out?

Destructive Habit #1: Expectations

This habit stems from our desires and often relies on a basic assumption that our partners would naturally do what we desire if they loved us or that they should know what we desire without us sharing it. An expectation is defined as a belief that someone *will* or *should* do or achieve something. Notice the "should" because it can be used as a red flag that allows you to recognize when you have any expectations. If you have it in your mind that someone *should* do something, it is very likely an expectation you have that stems from an underlying belief you hold. We often "should" on ourselves as well. You may be living out a belief you have taken on from your family or culture by making yourself do things that you expect a loving partner would do and this can cause you to feel resentment.

Even though it is rooted in your own belief or expectation, you may blame your partner for it. Instead, what if you let go of all your "shoulds" and turned them into "coulds"? Wouldn't that give you much more freedom and ease? Are you willing to find out? If so, play and explore with the following key practices

What if you let go of all your "shoulds" and turned them into "coulds"?

to shift out of expectations and into possibilities that will bring you and your partner into greater understanding, collaboration and closeness.

Key Shifting Practices: Requests and Explorations

When you notice that you have an expectation of your partner, the most magical turn-around is to turn the expectation into a request—a very specific and doable request.

Let's look at an example that came up in my own relationship: *It is a priority for me to stay warm enough because I feel physically and emotionally tense when I'm cold. So when I moved in with my partner, I had an expectation that knowing this about me, he would help keep the fire going during the night, since he wakes up more often than I do. However, this expectation didn't work very well for me because his body runs warmer and it's not a big deal for him if the house cools down a bit. He also had a small heater in his home office, so it was no problem for him to let the fire go out in the main house and start one in the morning, allowing the house to warm up while he was reading the daily news in his office. I'd wake up to no fire and a cold house that would take hours to warm up to a temperature that was comfortable for me, even with multiple layers of sweaters. So, after first being offended that he didn't care enough to keep me warm, (this was a clue to my underlying assumption or belief) I made a specific request. "Honey, so I can feel comfortable and relaxed during my morning yoga, would you help keep the fire going by putting a log on the fire when you get up during the night?" After that, he was much more conscious about keeping the fire going at all times. Notice that the request I made was very specific. I didn't just ask him to keep me warm, I gave him both the awareness of my experience and a specific way to support me. I also proactively took care of my own need for additional warmth by being sure to attend to the fire before going to bed. Through the exploration of my expectations, I became aware of my belief that if someone loves me, they will be attentive to my physical needs, in this case, my need for warmth. By letting go of this belief, I let go of my own suffering around it.*

In coaching both men and women, I have noticed that I am not the only one who has ever taken on the specific belief that someone who loves me will be attentive to my needs. I have seen that the people who love us may sometimes be aware of what gives us comfort and pleasure, and may not always notice our experience, even though they love us. Therefore, it is up to us to make the specific requests that honor what is most important to us and allow us to feel loved, adored and supported. Doing this prevents all sorts of tension, suffering and arguments while also giving us more opportunities to nourish the love we share by pleasing and being pleased.

When you discover that you have a "should" or an expectation, whether for yourself or your partner, you can unravel your expectations at their roots by exploring your underlying beliefs. Such exploration can be very revealing. Sometimes the underlying beliefs are unconscious beliefs from our past or ones that we've picked up from others that may not even be in alignment with what's true for us now. Once you uncover these limiting beliefs, you have an opportunity to choose again. At this point, you can make new choices based on your current preferences and priorities. How much more fun and fulfillment would that create in your relationship?

Destructive Habit #2: Assumptions and Judgments

Remember, the first step to shifting a pattern is to become aware of it. It's important to be aware of how our assumptions and judgments close doors to real communication and sharing. In fact, they can end the conversation altogether, if you shift into an internal monologue based on the stories you are fabricating in your head. Your inner monologue prevents you from seeing or hearing what's true in the moment or from considering any new options, cutting off dialogue and closing the doors on communication, connection and new possibilities. This builds a wall of distance between you and your partner that will destroy your relationship over time, not to mention the stressful effects of all the pain, drama and suffering this creates for you, both physically and emotionally.

So, how do we recognize our assumptions and judgments in time to prevent damage and suffering?

An assumption or supposition is something we imagine, project or presume to be true. Assumptions reflect our way of viewing or navigating the world when we imagine another being would feel, think, act, or respond as we do. Assumptions can also reflect judgments we've made. For instance, if we judge someone to be a certain kind of person, we might also have assumptions about how that person would feel, think, act or respond based on our judgment of him or her.

Judgments include opinions, conclusions and decisions in response to our perceptions or assumptions. As human beings, living in a predominantly dualistic culture, and often functioning as if in survival mode, our minds go into judgment habitually. We judge ourselves. We judge our partners. We judge actions, situations and people. We often judge reactively in response to our own fears and insecurities as a way to compartmentalize things that feel scary and get to the "case closed" position. Judging ourselves and each other is so normal to us that we often don't even realize we are doing it. And we do have a choice. In other words, we can shift this judgment habit in each moment of awareness.

Now, let's look at our judgment process to see the steps and points of choice we have along the way.

First, you have a perception or awareness of a situation, person or pattern. Then, you might respond to that awareness by adding a judgment. That judgment could be an opinion, conclusion or decision. Adding the judgment is a choice. Then you might draw more conclusions and make further decisions based on the first judgment. This last choice quickly spirals away from the original perception or awareness that you had. Without the judgment, you simply have the awareness. So, you could choose to simply notice or acknowledge what you perceive.

Here's an example to illustrate the judgment process:
You might notice that your partner hasn't arrived home from work and it's an hour past when he/she usually gets home. You could add to this awareness an opinion that your partner is wrong or bad for being late, or an assumption that your partner doesn't care about you otherwise she would have been on time, or you could conclude that your partner is having an affair.

I have exaggerated this example somewhat to make the pattern and choices more obvious. You probably get the point by now.

Sometimes we create stories or assumptions out of thin air. Sometimes we create them by projecting our inner fears outward. Often, we then use these stories and assumptions as the basis for more judgments. Can you see how quickly this could take us away from a real relationship with our partner and, instead, create a whole drama in our mind that has little or nothing at all to do with our partner? We can create a lot of pain and suffering for ourselves and in our relationships using our judgments and assumptions as weapons of destruction. And you don't need to judge yourself if you have this habit. As a human being myself, I know how easy it is to go there. *And* you have the power to make new choices starting right now.

First, would you be willing to let go of making yourself wrong or bad and instead give yourself a chance to just notice when you are judging and assuming? And once you notice, would you be willing to choose to do something much more fun and simple to turn this habit around? If you've said yes and yes, you are about to free yourself from a lot of pain, drama and suffering. Use the key practice I give you below to enjoy a new sense of freedom and lightness within yourself and in your relationships.

Key Shifting Practice: Being Curious

Being curious is one of the most creative choices we can make in our relationships and in our lives. We come into this world with curiosity. And it is our most natural and magical state of being, because it is pure, creative potential. This state of wonder and curiosity can be cultivated by asking questions. When I notice myself making a conclusion, I often ask, "What else is possible"? This question is my quick way to shift out of judgment and open up to the idea that there are other options beyond the one my mind first jumped on. "I wonder what choices I could make here that will create the closeness (or replace the word "closeness" with whatever it is that *you* are truly desiring) I desire?" When the judgment is about your partner, you can be curious and ask questions to discover what he/she is thinking, feeling, choosing or desiring instead. "Tell me more about that" is a great way to elicit more clarity from one another. In the example above, you might turn it around by replacing the story that jumped into your mind with becoming curious about it instead. The underlying qualities of curiosity are the essence of kindness, generosity, honoring and caring. Curiosity is a way of truly loving by choosing to know more about your partner's feelings, desires, preferences and being. Our spirit wants to experience connection by being seen, felt and heard. When you ask and listen deeply with curiosity to whatever wants to be expressed, you are giving one of the most precious gifts you can give to one you love.

Destructive Habit #3: Blame

The blaming habit takes you into a "powerless victim" position and leaves you helpless and hopeless in your relationship. It also sets up your partner as your enemy instead of your ally, creating a situation in which you are opposing each other, a scenario that's guaranteed to lead to distance and destruction. Blame is one of the most common toxic habits in our relationships. We usually go into blame when something isn't working for us or didn't turn out the way we

Being curious is one of the most creative choices we can make in our relationships and in our lives.

wanted. For those of us who may tend to blame and punish *ourselves*, blaming someone else is a way out that feels a bit better. For this same reason, blame goes hand in hand with an attachment to being right, the last destructive habit we will explore in this chapter. So where do you blame in your relationships? How does it show up? It doesn't have to be in your intimate relationship, it can be any relationship or even how you blame the world, blaming "them," blaming the government, whomever. How do you feel when you are thinking thoughts of blame? How does it affect your body and well-being? What if you don't have to blame anyone? What if you don't have to make you or anyone else wrong? What would feel even better than that? What else is possible?

Key Shifting Practices: Owning (self-ownership) and choosing (self-empowerment)

You can turn blame around by owning and taking responsibility for your feelings, actions and choices. I call this "self-ownership." *And*, by making new choices or taking different actions in order to get a new outcome that works better for you, which I call "self-empowerment." Adding in a bit of appreciation, as described in chapter 2, can also go a long way to help you shift out of the habit of blaming.

So, let's explore an example to make this clearer.

Joe was really upset at Beth because their dogs were disrupting their home. He said that he wanted a peaceful place to come home to after work and she had neglected to train the dogs, especially the newest puppy, so now they were wild around the house and barked much too much. In this scenario, Joe is blaming Beth for the situation with the dogs and feels justified because she is the one who originally wanted to have dogs, so she should have been the one to train them. Beth responds defensively. She loves the dogs and isn't bothered by their behavior. She finds it a bit entertaining even though she's aware that the barking irritates Joe and might disturb the neighbors, too. She says the dogs always get more rowdy when Joe comes home, and thinks that if he would relax about it and greet them with a little attention they wouldn't be as wild. Does this dynamic seem familiar? The cycle of blame and defensiveness would just keep building up between Joe and Beth if they didn't do something to turn it around. Even though there may be some truth in each of their perceptions, blaming each other won't lead to a solution, nor will it bring them any closer to each other. Just so we're clear that this is not about deciding who is right or wrong, let's explore how each of them might use the key practices of self-ownership and self-empowerment to turn this situation around.

Joe's turn-around:

Joe says to Beth, "I've been thinking about what I can do to shift my discomfort with the dogs and I've realized that I need to take responsibility for training them, since I'm the one with the issue. I'm going to look into some dog training programs that are scheduled on weekends when I'm not working."

Can you feel the energy shift in that? Powerful, eh? He's taking responsibility for his feelings and making a new choice that empowers him in the situation, while honoring Beth and clearing the blame that was creating a wall between them.

Beth's turn-around:

Beth says to Joe, "I see how the dogs' behavior doesn't support your need for a peaceful home. I'm also noticing that this is getting in the way of our connection and I feel sad about that. I've been wondering what I can do to shift this situation and I have a few ideas I'd like to explore. I think if the dogs had an outdoor area where they could play together and run off some of their energy, they would be more relaxed in the house. Would you be willing to help me create that?"

Summing up, Beth has acknowledged Joe's complaints, owned her own feelings and made a new choice to take some action to solve the problem, while also inviting Joe to co-create the solution with her. This means that they can both feel good about it!

You see, it doesn't matter so much who makes the first move to shift things. The important thing is to make the shift as soon as you become aware of it, because attachment to blaming, or holding onto the anger, or clinging to being right will all lead to irreparable damage eventually.

Another practice that relieves the internal suffering and shifts the energy of blame to create profound results is the *forgiveness practice* you will find at the end of this chapter.

Destructive Habit #4: Clinging to Being Right

When you cling to being right, you need to make someone else wrong in order to *prove* that you're right. When you do this in your relationship, that "someone" is usually your partner.

How do you feel when someone makes you wrong? Defensive? Competitive? Resistant? Disconnected? Does it ever draw you closer? Do you feel loved, adored, seen, felt or heard in the right-wrong tug of war?

When you cling to being right, it is as if you are building a cement wall between you and your partner. Every time you cling to a rightness, you are adding another block of cement to the wall between you. This will often inspire your partner to resist by proving how she is right, too, or by defending herself against being wrong. It becomes a vicious cycle that is difficult to interrupt and contributes to building the wall that is growing between you. Eventually there is no getting over the wall of distance and destruction you have created.

You may have heard this classic and powerful question: "Do you want to be right or do you want to be happy"? I would also ask: "Do you want to be right or do you want love and connection"? What if you choose love and happiness over being right and stop making you or anyone else wrong? How would that feel in your body and in your heart?

Key Shifting Practices: Choosing love and happiness instead of being right.

Every time you take a position, attitude or perspective you are choosing it, *and* you have an option to choose something different. You may be choosing it unconsciously. And you'll know this because it usually feels as if it is the *only* option, rather than being a choice. So, the first step to turn this around is to become aware of and to acknowledge the position, attitude or perspective you are choosing, and to notice the impact it's having on your connection with your partner. Then ask yourself the questions I mentioned earlier.

Question 1: The first question is: "Do I want to be right or do I want love and connection"? If you want love and connection, then you'll have to let go of needing to be right. But you don't need to make yourself wrong, either. You can just choose a position that embraces both you and your partner even if you have different preferences or points of view. It's okay not to agree on everything. Having different ideas and perspectives has many advantages, including that it's just more interesting than if we were all the same. It also gives us a chance to co-create solutions that neither of us would likely have come up with on our own. You'll learn all the specific steps of how to do that in the Co-creating Solutions Process in chapter 9. Allowing yourself and your partner to be and express all of who you are is a great gift that invites you to touch this world and each other in the way that only you can. Isn't that what we are all here to enjoy? Being. Expressing. Receiving. Touching and being touched.

Happiness is a choice. And you are the only one who can choose happiness for you.

Question 2: Now let's get to the second question because it's an important one. "Do you want to be right or do you want to be happy?" If you desire happiness, I'm here to support you. First, you have to choose it. Happiness is a choice. And you are the only one who can choose happiness for you. If you don't want to be happy, nobody else can make you *be* happy. You get to choose happiness again at any moment. At the end of this chapter, you'll find some tools you can use when you're choosing happiness. I'll give you my top three Happiness Tools. These tools have worked time after time to help me and my coaching clients to shift into a lighter, happier state of being.

Questions to ask:

Asking questions opens you to new solutions and possibilities. No need to know or find the answers. Just ask the question with curiosity, speaking out loud if possible, and then release it. Be open to new insights and possibilities. Stay tuned to what shows up. Guidance may come instantly or later. It may come as new awareness, feelings, thoughts, images, or in other forms. Asking questions opens the door to miracles.

What else is possible?

What assumptions or judgments am I holding that I can turn into curiosity right now?

What story do I have running in my mind? Do I have fear attached to the story?

What am I afraid of right now?

What if I embrace myself and my fear with understanding?

Who am I blaming that I could choose to forgive right now?

What am I blaming someone or something for that I could take responsibility for now?

How much more generous, kind and loving can I be with myself and my Love right now?

What if I choose happiness over being right and stop making me or anyone else wrong?

Do I want to be right or do I want love and connection?

Do I want to be right or do I want to be happy?

What's the blessing in this that I'm not seeing?

What can I choose to nourish my own peace, fun and joy in this moment?

What "shoulds" or resentments do I have that can give me clues to expectations I hold?

What old beliefs or assumptions can I uncover in those expectations? And what new choices and clear requests can I make now?

Tools and practices to use:

1) Happiness Tool #1 is to focus on the full half of the cup rather than the empty half. In other words, focus on what brings you joy in your life or celebrate what is working well instead of looking for what's wrong. When you get stuck, ask yourself questions such as: "What can I be grateful for in this moment?" or "What's the blessing in this?" or "How does it get any better than this?" Even during a sad or tragic time, you can ask a question like: "What's the gift in this that I'm not seeing?" This allows room within you for those blessings in disguise. This simple age-old wisdom is the secret that has allowed people to find happiness in the hardest situations, and if you use this happiness tool regularly, it will change your life!

Here's a story to illustrate the power of choosing happiness in a scary moment:

When I go on a road trip, I like to leave in the wee hours of the morning to get ahead of traffic and for the pleasure and renewed energy I receive as the sun rises. On the day in this story, I was traveling solo and had the breakfast frittata I had packed for myself on the dashboard warming up in the sun. As I took a turn onto an on ramp, my breakfast went

continued...

Tools and practices to use continued

flying and I reached over to catch it as I steered right off the road and stopped just in time. I now sat with my little Honda peeking over the edge of a small cliff. Quite shaken up and scared, yet relieved that we didn't go over the edge, I took a couple of deep breaths and asked out loud, "How does it get even better than this?" Then I carefully crawled out the passenger side of my car to safety. Assessing the situation, I felt immensely grateful to discover that my car seemed undamaged. It was, however, in quite a precarious position and in need of a winch. Simultaneously celebrating my good fortune and inviting in even more, I asked the question again, "How does it get even better than this?" Then a miracle happened. A tow truck pulled up and the driver hopped out, saying: "Let's get your car out of there." He hooked it up and asked me to get back in the car to assist in the maneuver. As he began pulling, we seemed to be moving more toward the edge. At that point I lost it! He may have been certain of a positive outcome but I was terrified that my car and I were about to go over so I screamed for him to stop. Seeing my terror, he adjusted his approach so that I did not need to be inside and pulled my car safely back on the road. Then he came to comfort me, patiently holding my hand while I sobbed in release and relief. That kind, gentle man would not let me go until he was certain I was in a good state for driving. Finally, he sent me off with care and blessings, telling me that the charges were covered. I still made it to my retreat reunion dinner that evening, a bit later than planned, yet safe and sound.

2) Happiness Tool #2 is to shift into gratitude, pausing to give thanks for specific things you enjoy or feel blessed by in life, one by one. I often do this Gratitude Practice out loud when I'm driving alone and by the time I arrive wherever I'm going I'm in such a state of love and happiness that everyone is delighted to see me. In the context of your relationship, this practice may be pausing to notice what you feel grateful for relative to your partner. When you are overflowing with gratitude in your thoughts and in your heart, it will uplift your energy enough to have a positive impact on your partner, even if you don't say anything out loud. And sharing some of your gratitude in words can be a sweet bonus if you feel inspired to do so.

3) Happiness Tool #3 is to do something that you know brings you joy. It may be taking time in nature. It may be to move your body in some way. It may be to do something creative that allows you to express yourself. These three examples commonly take most people to a greater level of joy. Just do any or all of them that call to you.

continued...

Tools and practices to use continued

4) Forgiveness Practice:

Always start your forgiveness practice by forgiving your-self first. Here's the format:

I, (your name), forgive myself for any way I have hurt myself, or (name of a person you are choosing to forgive) or anyone else.

Say the forgiveness vow slowly, out loud, with heart-felt intentions. Say it at least three times or until you feel a shift. Next, move your attention to another person you wish to forgive and follow this format:

I, (your name), forgive (name of a person you are choosing to forgive) for any way she/he has hurt me, or herself/himself or anyone else.

Again, say it out loud three times or until you feel a shift, speaking slowly and with intent to forgive and release.

Then move on to the next person who comes to mind. Continue until no one else comes to mind and you feel complete.

The beauty of these specific forgiveness scripts is that they address the unconscious aspects of blame, including that we are probably blaming or shaming ourselves internally and that when we hurt someone else, we are almost always hurting ourselves as well. In this way we also acknowledge that the same is likely to be true for the one we need to forgive.

Do this forgiveness practice every day, ideally morning and evening before bed, and whenever you feel yourself holding a grudge of anger, resentment or blame toward anyone, including yourself.

This is a life-long practice. Stay with this daily forgiveness ritual until you no longer find yourself blaming anyone for anything and you feel empty of resentments. Then you can take a break from the practice until the next time you experience blame or resentment, and simply bring back the daily ritual.

Forgiveness and gratitude are my two most powerful practices for restoring inner peace, and opening up the free flow of love and joy. I find, now, that after doing the forgiveness practice for a few days, I am free of blame and grudges for a while. Then whenever a new or old one arises, I start the practice again until I feel clear and free once more. My clients have also reported profound shifts and wonderful feelings of joy and lightness from this practice.

Please also note: Forgiveness has nothing to do with condoning unacceptable or abusive behavior. We can forgive and simultaneously maintain clear, healthy boundaries.

Actions to choose:

This is simply a list of actions based on this chapter that you might choose to take on your proactive path. I offer them as options to support you in bringing the material from this manual to life. You may choose one or more from this list or you may find something else from the chapter that inspires your action. The practices work miracles when practiced! And to enjoy the shifts and miracles, you'll need to take actions!

continued...

Actions to choose continued

Action 1: Choose a tool or practice from this chapter to apply in your daily life. Choose one that resonates with you, as a starting point. Once you practice, explore and integrate that first one, then you might add another one, and so on.

Action 2: Choose just a few questions to ask from the lists at the end of each chapter to write on sticky notes and post them in places where you'll see them often. Choose questions that inspire you to make shifts in the direction of the new choices and outcomes you desire. Each time you see one of your posted questions, pause and ask it out loud if possible, or silently if necessary. Remember to breathe and allow the question to resonate for a moment. Keep asking and stay open for guidance and miracles to come.

Action 3: Start a journal to expand your awareness of your own patterns with these four destructive habits. Set aside a time for journaling each day. Looking back over the last twenty-four hours, when did you have expectations, assumptions, judgments or blame? When did you cling to being right? How and how soon did you recognize the pattern? Celebrate the recognition even if you're just having it now. How can you have fun noticing it a bit sooner next time? Were you able to turn it around? If so, woo-hoo! Celebrate your shift. If not, what could you have done to turn it around? Remember the first step is just to become aware of the patterns and that's the main purpose of this journaling. Then start playing with how you might do the turn around using the key shifting practices. Have fun with it!

Oh, and I want to mention here that it may be tempting to focus on how someone else, maybe even your partner, is playing out these habits. Being aware of the patterns is helpful, while pointing a finger is not so helpful. So, if you want to share your new awareness and discoveries, I invite you to use the key shifting practices of self-ownership and self-empowerment.

Action 4: Practice being curious and asking questions.

Bonus action: Write to me with your love miracles and I will celebrate each and every one! You will also be contributing to our love evolution movement by creating an expanding culture of healthy, thriving relationships in the world. I am exhilarated and motivated by your love miracle stories and the extraordinary results that unfold when you implement these simple yet powerful practices into your life.

Celebrations!

Celebrate every time you make a shift, have a new awareness or insight, make a new choice, take an action in alignment with what you desire or experience a miracle. Celebrations can be as simple as pausing to acknowledge a shift with a deep breath and a smile, a dance of joy, a hoot and a holler, sharing your success with a loved one or anything else that feels like fun and acknowledges the shifts and miracles taking place, whether small or huge.

4

Navigating Our Issues and Challenges with Grace

Creating a Safe Haven for Our Growth and Unfolding

Issues, challenges and the gift of awareness

ONE OF THE GIFTS, AND ALSO ONE OF THE CHALLENGES, of our love relationships is that they assist us in our evolution and growth as human beings by giving us chances for greater awareness. The people with whom we interact are like mirrors reflecting back to us how we are showing up. However, we may not always like or feel happy with the reflections we receive. Issues, bumps and challenges will naturally arise in our intimate connections, even in the presence of love, trust and healthy commitments. Each bump or challenge offers us a perfect opportunity to deepen our level of intimacy, while allowing us to grow and evolve both individually and together. If, instead of judging yourself, your partner or your relationship as being wrong or bad, you are willing to make more empowering choices, then you can discover the blessings that your issues and challenges offer.

Each bump or challenge offers us a perfect opportunity to deepen our level of intimacy, while allowing us to grow and evolve both individually and together.

You might start with the empowering choice to be curious about and then to take responsibility for your feelings, actions and interactions. If you are willing, you can make the empowering choice to learn and to change what isn't working and discover new options that may bring you even greater fun, fulfillment and closeness.

Allowing your feelings to direct your awareness

The key to opening this gateway to love is to give attention to those uneasy feelings that let us know we are unhappy with the reflections we are receiving or the kinds of interactions we are having. This may require slowing down enough to acknowledge to yourself, and then maybe also to your partner, when you are having those uneasy feelings. If this is new for you, you may be wondering how you could possibly give time and attention to the feelings that arise for you and your dear ones and still be able to do all the things you do in your day.

First, I want to let you know that if you create space in which to pause, you don't need a lot of time to give those feelings your full attention. It can take just the amount of time it takes for a few deep breaths. Second, for most of us, it will take less time than the time we devote to distracting ourselves from our uneasy feelings. Giving attention to your feelings, especially your uneasy feelings, may be outside your comfort zone. Believe me, I understand completely. *My* uneasy feelings are outside my comfort zone, too. I have also learned that giving these feelings my own attention and being curious about myself and my partner consistently leads me to the ease, closeness and comfort I really desire. On the other hand, ignoring the feelings usually takes me farther and farther away from the comfort and connection I choose to create.

I have also come up with some strategies that make it easier for me to make the healthy and rewarding choice of tuning into my feelings, comfortable or not, allowing them to direct my awareness. The first is to create the safety within myself and within our relationship to welcome and acknowledge all feelings. Making this commitment in your relationship is pivotal in creating and deepening intimacy. Creating this safe haven for shared vulnerability allows and inspires us to give attention to our feelings and to receive the true gifts of awareness and guidance our feelings give us in return.

The second strategy will be familiar, I'm sure. Simply, practice. As with most things, the more we do it, the easier it gets. I find that integrating this practice of feeling and sharing into our daily lives makes a big difference in the level of ease for both of us. It can become as natural as regular exercise, meditation or brushing and flossing your teeth. I have also noticed that, as with many things, when I get out of practice, I have to go through that initial hurdle to get going again.

Becoming collaborators and creating a safe haven together

What if you felt safe enough to be and express all of you? What if you could be completely you and feel all you feel and never be wrong? What if you and your partner hold your relationship as a safe haven for being and feeling without judging each other? What if you choose to be collaborators in this adventure of life by giving each other the grace and total allowance to be, feel, express, grow and evolve?

You can!

You and your partner co-create your relationship with or without awareness. *With awareness*, you can create whatever you choose together. You can be collaborators in whatever ways you choose. You might begin with an invitation to explore what kind of safety you'd each like to create in your relationship. What would a new commitment to being collaborators and creating safety do for you and your relationship?

Mis-takes and Mends

How might you allow grace in your relationship for mending, soothing and learning from the mis-takes that are a natural part of our human evolution?

Sometimes we do or say something that has a hurtful or damaging impact on one we love. If we had a chance to do it over again, we might choose to do or say it differently. What could give us that chance? How can we mend our wounds and restore trust and connection?

Apologies are one approach. And did you know that the meanings of the word "apology" includes explanation, justification and defense—which is exactly how many apologies go awry? Justifications and defensiveness usually add insult to injury, so they are especially important elements to leave out of any attempts to soothe or mend.

Owning our mis-takes is essential to making amends. It allows us to honor our perfectly imperfect human selves without needing to be wrong or bad. Honoring the impact of your words or actions on your loved one can restore trust and closeness, while being willing to make amends expresses your commitment to the well-being of your relationship and offers a chance to soothe the hurt or mend the damages.

On the flip side, when your partner says or does something that affects your level of trust or closeness, it serves the quality of your connection and the health of your relationship to express what you're experiencing as an invitation to deepen your intimate connection and understanding of each other.

When we make the same mis-take again, I call it a rerun. Multiple reruns can be like salt in a wound and may be slower to mend. To prevent reruns as well as to soothe hurts and mend damage, it is important to address our issues and mis-takes as they arise.

Owning our mis-takes is essential to making amends.

Here are the three key elements for mending your "mis-takes." They are presented in a step-by-step format with some samples and language considerations to assist you.

Step 1: Own your feelings and actions.

I made a mis-take when I _____. (Be specific)

I felt out of alignment when I _____. (Be specific)

I feel sad about the choice I made when I... (Be specific)

I regret how I handled that. May I have a do-over?

I regret doing or saying ____. (Be specific)

Oh dear, I didn't handle that very gracefully. Take 2...(Humor & lightness can bring grace & ease, when appropriate.)

My mis-take. Please allow me to re-do that.

Words are powerful, so I invite you to choose your words carefully. Be specific and honest. Don't say something just because you think it's what your partner wants to hear, especially if it's not your truth. Not speaking your truth will not make a real mend and will even worsen the situation. Express what is authentic, true and in alignment for you.

Here's an example:
For me, the word "sorry" has a weighed-down energy. Its meanings include sorrowful, ashamed, pitiful, and miserable, which rarely describe an expression of my authentic self. Also," I am" statements have an especially potent effect as affirmations. So, I

have added the phrase, "I'm sorry" to my evolving list of words and phrases that I am gradually clearing out of my vocabulary. This is one of the more challenging ones to clear since the phrase is so heavily used in our culture and I've had many years of hearing and speaking it. "Mistake," on the other hand, has a much lighter energy to me, and a "mis- take" sounds as if it invites the possibility for a "new take" or a "do-over." To align with this higher vibrational possibility, I prefer to own *my mis-takes rather than to "be sorry." Exploring and being conscious of your choice of words is simply another opportunity to expand your awareness and become even more true to yourself.*

Step 2: Acknowledge the impact your actions have had on your partner and your relationship. Your original intentions may have been a sincere attempt to do something kind and loving for your partner or yourself, and sometimes sharing your true intentions can soothe the hurt if you also fully acknowledge the real impact your actions have had. However, be very mindful of a tendency to defend, explain or justify. These are self-protective strategies you are using to hold on to being right or to avoid taking full responsibility for your mis-take. As such, they will more than likely add insult to injury, widening the gap and the damages between you and your partner.

I feel heavy in my heart now that I know how (name what you said or did) impacted (you/us/our relationship).

I see how (doing or saying) _____ led to _____(whatever problem ensued).

I know now how (doing or saying) _____ contributed to you feeling (hurt or _____).

I regret doing or saying _____ because of the impact (or better yet, name the specific impact) it has had on (you/us/our relationship).

Step 3: Express your desire to soothe and mend. You might also ask for a new take or ask for forgiveness.
Please forgive me. What can I do that would honor you more?

Please forgive me. How can I restore your trust or make amends or_____?

How can I handle this in a way that would feel better to you?

What can I do or offer to soothe or comfort you now?

What can I do to mend this (if possible name the specific wound or damage your partner is expressing)?

Oh dear! That was not what I meant to say at all. Let's erase that and start over. (when appropriate and you have access to playfulness and lightness)

As you practice this dance of intimacy together, at times you'll be able to catch your mis-takes and blunders in the hot little moments when you are making them and be able to correct your course of action or take a do-over right then.

Questions to ask:

Asking questions opens us to new possibilities and solutions. No need to know or find the answers. Just ask the question with a sense of curiosity, speaking out loud if possible, and then release it. Be open to new insights and possibilities. Stay tuned to what shows up. Guidance may come instantly or later. It may come as new awareness, feelings, thoughts, images, or in other forms. Asking opens the door to miracles.

What if I choose happiness over being right and stop making me or anyone else wrong?

What if I allow myself to feel all I feel without making me or anyone else wrong?

What if I choose to see our issues and challenges as opportunities for deeper connection and self-empowerment?

What kind of safe haven would support me most to explore my own feelings right now?

How can I create safe haven for myself right now?

How can I create safe haven within myself right now?

How can I create safe haven for my partner right now?

How can we navigate our issues and challenges together in a way that allows us to grow and evolve, becoming even better people?

What would a new commitment to being collaborators change for me? for my partner? for our relationship?

What if I receive my partner with total allowance to be, feel, express, grow and evolve?

Questions to ask continued

How can I invite more grace into my relationships and interactions?

How can I be even more open to owning and learning from my mis-takes as a natural part of my growth and evolution?

How can I honor my perfectly imperfect human self without needing to be wrong or bad?

How can we create even more safety together to invite more honesty, openness and closeness in our relationship?

How can we create our relationship as a safe haven for being and feeling without judging each other?

What mis-takes can I take action to mend now?

Tools and practices to use:

1) Tuning In to Your Feelings Practice:

By tuning in to your feelings you can receive the messages and guidance they offer. Your light and happy feelings let you know when things are in alignment for you while uneasy feelings let you know when something is out of alignment for you. These are all messages worth listening to.

Uneasy feelings usually signal that something needs to be noticed or addressed. So let's start there. Whenever you become aware of an uneasy feeling, take a moment to pause and breathe and be curious about it. Allow your breath to deepen and simply notice where the uneasy feeling resides within your body. Breathe into that place and ask the question, "What triggered this feeling in me?" You may be feeling uneasy about a thought or interaction you've just had. Then ask: "What about that feels scary or uncomfortable to me?" Or "What judgment am I having about that?" and "What conclusion did I draw from that?" You may be able to identify the feeling as well. Check in and be curious. Are you feeling sad? Hurt? Angry? Afraid? Ashamed? Use your uneasy feelings as a way of gathering information about yourself. Once you practice this step a few times and have more awareness of what's going on inside you, you may want to take the next step of sharing your awareness. Cultivating this practice of listening deeply to the messages your feelings provide will save you a lot of pain and suffering, as they guide you to make choices that are in alignment for you.

continued...

Tools and practices to use continued

2) Be Your Safe Haven Practice:

Here's a way to create more safety for yourself that extends safety into your relationships. When you become the safety you require, you create a safe haven you can rely on even when others seem unreliable. Though this practice is simple, it is definitely a stretch for most of us. And it is so incredibly worth it! So just do your best. Here's how: Begin treating yourself the way you most want to be treated. Give yourself the kind, caring, non-judgmental attention you would give to a dear one who was feeling vulnerable. Become a steady presence for yourself. And here's the sweetest part. Look at yourself in the mirror with the same loving eyes with which you would see an adorable child. Now talk to that child, offering love and encouragement. Say the things that will help your inner child feel safe. Most of us are afraid of criticism, abandonment and rejection. So say things such as, "I see you." "I'm here for you. I'm not going anywhere. I'm right here." "I love you." Speak from your heart. Even if this is way beyond your comfort zone, I promise the practice gets easier the more you do it. And if you're feeling tender, you will almost certainly cry a good cry.

Actions to choose:

This is simply a list of actions based on this chapter that you might choose to take on your proactive path. I offer them as options to support you in bringing the material from this manual to life. You may choose one or more from this list or you may find something else from the chapter that inspires your action. The practices work miracles when practiced! And to enjoy the shifts and miracles, you'll need to take actions!

Action 1: Make a commitment to being a collaborator with your partner.

Action 2: Review the sections and practices in chapter 2 regarding opening the Gates of Love with the Key of Courageous Communication. The material of this chapter goes hand in hand with Courageous Communication.

Action 3: With an activity partner, practice the scripts in the mis-takes and mends section. You can take turns creating scenarios or using real situations. Be yourself in the scenario or situation and ask your practice partner to play the role of the other people involved. Notice and share the feelings that come up as you try on the scripts. Notice how you feel when you are owning, acknowledging, soothing and mending. And when you are playing the other role, be aware of and share your authentic feelings and responses. Allow the experience to be as real as possible.

continued...

Actions to choose continued

Action 4: Take time right now to do the "Be Your Safe Haven Practice" from the "Tools and practices to use" section above.

Action 5: Take time right now to do the "Tuning into Your Feelings Practice" from the "Tools and practices to use" section above.

Bonus action: Write to me with your love miracles and I will celebrate each and every one! You will also be contributing to our love evolution movement by creating an expanding culture of healthy, thriving relationships in the world. I am exhilarated and motivated by your love miracle stories and the extraordinary results that unfold when you implement these simple yet powerful practices into your life.

Celebrations!

Celebrate every time you make a shift, have a new awareness or insight, make a new choice, take an action in alignment with what you desire or experience a miracle. Celebrations can be as simple as pausing to acknowledge a shift with a deep breath and a smile, a dance of joy, a hoot and a holler, sharing your success with a loved one or anything else that feels fun and acknowledges the shifts and miracles taking place, whether small or huge.

5

Your First Love is You

Self Care Practices for Thriving in Love and Life

Waterfalls and deserts

I OFTEN FEEL AS THOUGH MY HEART IS OVERFLOWING like a waterfall of love. When I am living in this state of being I am fully alive and thriving. Love and blessings come to me naturally and life flows easily. I am inspired, motivated and energized. I can accomplish much and receive pleasure from the journey.

This waterfall of love flows from feeling nourished physically, emotionally and spiritually.

Take a moment to remember a time when you have experienced a similar feeling of overflowing love. What led you to that state of being? Do you remember how you opened up that abundant flow of love within, through and to you?

If you can't remember a time when you've felt such an abundant flow of love, this chapter is especially for you. It will likely stretch you into unfamiliar territory and you may even find it uncomfortable at first. However, if you allow yourself to stretch and experiment in some radically new ways, the rewards will be profound for you. If you haven't already done so, read the Introduction, "How to receive the most from this book", and follow the suggestions to receive the most from this chapter.

This waterfall of love flows from feeling nourished physically, emotionally and spiritually. When your thoughts, choices and actions are in alignment with love as a priority in your life, the streams of love flow naturally in ways that continue to replenish you.

When my coaching clients complain of a lack of love, further investigation often reveals that, though there may be room to expand the love being shared, they are actually missing the love that is there and available already, simply because they are not able to receive it. Two factors contribute to this. One is that the love is being given in a form they don't recognize. And two, they have become so drained and depleted, dry and barren that the flow of love simply runs off without sinking in. In other words, it is not being received. Since our world reflects back to us what we are being and expressing, this drought is not likely to encourage or invite more love, but is more likely to discourage the flow of love from others, who may feel as if they are watering a desert.

If you are unable to receive love, it reduces the outward love flow as well. To truly give love to another, you need to have enough love flowing through you to share. It's a bit like putting on your own oxygen mask before you assist another. If you pass out from a lack of air, you won't be able to help someone else to a steady flow of air, so you will be doing everyone a favor when you take care of your own oxygen flow. It is worth noting that if loving someone else leaves you feeling drained and depleted, it is likely to become a downward spiral for both of you. So, do everyone a favor and take a look to see what's really going on and what you need to shift to be replenished.

Ways to nourish and replenish yourself that open up the flow of love

For you to feel loved, you need to be able to receive the love that's there, from all of its many sources, including from within yourself. The first step is to choose and commit to nourishing and replenishing yourself to open up the natural flow of love and well-being within, through and to you. You may have ways that you do this already. If so, this chapter will give you more practices to enrich and expand your flow of love. Doing these practices will allow you to receive the love that is already available, as you become more in love with yourself and more in love with life. And you may even find yourself filled to overflowing like a waterfall.

Note: As a culture, we have many ways of avoiding our feelings, including the use of substances like stimulants, alcohol and sugar. These practices are designed to help us become more aware of our feelings and more present with ourselves. So plan to do these practices without using substances, which would defeat the purpose and undermine your desired results.

Giving yourself some loving attention

We all need love and attention. And one of the best ways to begin to open up the flow of giving and receiving love is to give and receive some of your own loving attention. This is a simple practice and it may seem silly or awkward at first since most of us have not been raised to love ourselves. Self love is one of the essential foundations of healthy people and relationships, so once you get some love flowing for yourself, feel free to start sharing this practice with all the young ones in your life. Wouldn't it be a much more loving world if we all learned this practice in our early formative years?

A loving attention practice: You might want to prime the pump by first remembering a time when you were in love with someone, whether it was one of your parents or your partner or your child or even a pet. Remember how you felt when you looked at them. Now, take a moment to see, notice and appreciate yourself as you would if you were observing a loved one. See yourself through loving eyes. Notice how you are being and expressing in this moment. Notice your body language, your attitude, your gestures. Tune into your strength and your vulnerability. Notice what you appreciate about yourself and what you find harder to accept. Love it all. Embrace yourself in your own love energy. You might even give voice to your love and appreciation just as you might speak to a dear one. Practice saying, "I love you," to yourself. Say it out loud, if possible, and see if you can even say it as you look into your own eyes in the mirror.

Physical self-care and nourishment

After witnessing and working with many people over the past thirty years, I have noticed again and again that people will neglect their basic survival needs like sleep and nutrition and still expect themselves and each other to be able to show up for their relationships. I find this especially amazing because I can't even show up for myself, let alone someone else, in a present and balanced way when I'm sleep deprived or low blood sugar. In fact, these are pretty much the rare times I am likely to lose my temper or fall apart in a sudden flow of tears. My Love, my friends and my family all know that I prioritize regular meals and a good night's rest because it just doesn't serve anyone if I don't. Now, you may not be as affected by this as I am or you may not be aware of the degree of impact that these basic needs are having on the quality of your mood, attitude and attention. I have helped many people dramatically reduce the frequency and pitch of arguments by becoming aware of how these basic needs impact their moods and reactivity and therefore their relationships.

Here's an experimental approach you can follow to find out whether this is having an impact on you and your relationships.

Learning to listen: First begin charting the qualities of your moods, attitudes and focus as well as your bedtime, quality and hours of sleep each night, the beverages you drink and the foods

Notice what you appreciate about yourself and what you find harder to accept. Love it all.

and times you eat each day. Do this for at least three weeks and see if you notice any patterns. Then begin to improve one area of your physical self-care and nourishment as you continue charting and see what you discover. Your body will tell you everything you need to know. I applied this experimental approach of charting, discovering patterns and making improvements for several years and it changed my life! I was able to recover from a long list of ailments and find my way to radiant health after many years of suffering through my teens and early twenties. It started with a choice and a commitment to self-care "to do whatever it takes to feel fabulous every day." We create whatever we are committed to creating. So if you want to create something even better, simply choose again and create a new commitment.

Nourishing foods: Give yourself three to five healthy, nutritional meals per day with the objective of replenishing your mind and body as well as enjoying the sensual pleasure of each meal. Invite more vibrancy and pleasure to unfold beyond your culinary delight by allowing yourself to stop eating while you're still a little hungry. Eating to the point of feeling completely full will often slow you down rather than pick you up while simultaneously dulling rather than stimulating your senses. You can do an experiment, to find out what degree of fullness keeps your senses most vivid and alive, by taking several deep breaths after your meals and tuning into your physical and emotional sensations. To enjoy sustained energy, eat whole foods instead of refined foods. Sugar and refined flour foods like bread, crackers and pasta are likely to create moodiness in most people and spikes of hyperactivity or reactivity followed by energetic lethargy and emotional lows. Charting is the best way to know how your choices are working for you.

Rest and relaxation: Sleep or rest when you are tired. Remember the wisdom of kindergarten and summer camp. Five-minute to fifteen-minute naps can be very rejuvenating. If your current schedule doesn't allow your body to get its rest requirements, consider what you might be able to shift in order to get enough R&R. It is common wisdom in many healing traditions that the most replenishing sleep for human beings occurs between the hours of 9 PM and midnight. I find that going to sleep by 10 PM consistently cultivates deeply restful sleep and enhances vitality. At about 11 PM, our body reboots, so I notice that if I'm not asleep by then, I get a second wind and I'm up for at least an hour if not more. Also, if you're tired all the time, it may be that you've been pushing yourself on low sleep or too much caffeine or both. You may need to replenish yourself a bit before you are able to find what would be a naturally balanced sleep schedule.

Physical exercise: Physical exercise can give you some personal time, refresh your mind, boost your confidence, and restore your spirits, as well as all the other physical health benefits like strengthening muscles and bones, maintaining ideal weight and boosting your energy. Options include walking or hiking, running, riding, swimming, Pilates, yoga, dancing (even in your living room), physical work like gardening or chopping wood, sports—you name it.

Coming into alignment with yourself

Essentially, this means to be consciously choosing and acting in accordance with what is most important to you. A myriad of practices are available that you can use to keep yourself on your own personal path to your heart's desires. A foundational step that I often guide my coaching clients through is to clarify your values, purpose and vision for your life and use this as a map to inform your choices to keep you on your chosen path. When you lose sight of these things, your path will meander as well. I have seen this operating in my own life and relationships.

Whatever I prioritize and put my attention toward creates the difference between direct manifestation and traveling the long, winding
road. Research has shown that where our minds go we follow, so
if we are celebrating our blessings, while holding the life vision we
dream of creating, we will move toward our blessings and visions.
However, when our thoughts (within ours minds or expressed) are
focused on what's wrong instead of toward our desired vision, we
will continue in the direction of what's not working and be moving
away from the realization of our dreams.

The first step of coming into alignment with yourself is to pause
and notice your thoughts, choices and actions throughout the
day, checking in often to see if they are lining up together and
in keeping with what you truly desire. If not, or not always,
begin to cultivate ways to shift the thoughts, choices or actions
that are out of alignment for you in whatever way you need to
so that you can get yourself back on course. Many peace and
well-being practices, as described later in this chapter, can help
you make these shifts. Whenever you check in and find your
thoughts, choices and actions are aligned together in moving
toward your desires, let yourself celebrate and enjoy the magic
and miracles of being in alignment!

Making friends with your feelings

Cultivating your capacity to feel and listen to the wisdom and
messages within your feelings is a book topic in itself. The
inability to process your feelings or the feelings of a loved one
is often the limiting factor that leads to keeping love at bay,
while embracing them can enrich the love and closeness you
are able to feel.

Your feelings are your friends and guides. They highlight what's
going on inside of you. Usually feelings of fun and lightness will

lead the way toward your desires while painful, heavy feelings let you know something is calling for your attention and you may be moving away from what you truly desire. It is immensely helpful to be able to receive all the valuable information and guidance your feelings can provide. In addition to providing navigational assistance on your chosen path, improving your emotional literacy will deeply enhance your capacity to give and receive love. Here, I will introduce just a couple of ways to practice feeling.

Feeling practice #1: Becoming acquainted with your feelings. Create time in each day to breathe, feel and check in with yourself. Commit to setting aside 5- 15 minutes for this feeling practice. Allow yourself to sit comfortably in stillness. You might wish to rest one hand on your heart and one on your belly, or you could simply rest your hands in your lap. Allow yourself to drop in by deepening your breath, becoming aware of the breath as it flows in and out. Begin to scan your body starting at your toes and moving up toward your head, slowly, to notice how each and every part of your body feels. You may notice places that feel tired or energized, empty or full, or tingly or yummy or achy. Notice where you feel at ease in your body and where you feel tension or discomfort and anything else you feel. Now choose a place in your body to focus on. Choose an area that is easier for you to tune into. This is likely to be one with more noticeable sensations or as I usually say, "a place in your body that is speaking more loudly." Give this area your loving attention, the kind of attention you might give a child who needs some TLC. Be curious and loving toward it. How does it feel? How big is the area of sensation? What emotions do you feel as you breathe into it? Give your love to all the feelings that arise and love yourself as you feel them.

Feeling practice #2: Befriending your feelings

You can do this as a practice of connecting with yourself, and as a way of connecting and sharing with your partner as well. Below you will see the four most basic feelings that we cycle through in our human moments: happy, sad, angry and fearful. By learning to recognize, befriend and express these four feelings, we enhance our capacity for navigating our own emotions and those felt by loved ones. Most of us have feelings we are in touch with, the ones that are easy or acceptable to us, and others we suppress or submerge because we judge them or find them uncomfortable to be with. It is common for some of us to go to anger and avoid the feelings of fear or sadness beneath the anger, while others among us may go to sadness and avoid anger. In this practice you'll get to cultivate a greater awareness of your feelings so you can receive the gifts and guidance they offer.

Visit with each feeling by asking and answering the questions associated with it. Answer each question with one, simple sentence. Leave out the story, explanations or reasons and just get in touch with the feeling as you speak or write the answer. Here's an example: "I felt fearful about telling my partner that the rear view mirror of his car broke off when I adjusted it today. I was afraid he would be angry at me for breaking it." You can write your answers on a sheet of paper, or in your journal or share it with your partner or a friend with whom you've agreed to practice. Notice where and how you feel each feeling in your body. If you do this practice with someone else, it is best, at first, to get used to sharing feelings around situations that don't involve your practice partner. As you gain comfort with simply sharing and listening to each other's feelings, then you can advance to doing so even when the feelings being shared are related to each other. You will know you are ready for this more advanced version when you are able to allow each other to have any feeling. While you listen to your partner's sharing, you'll also have feelings of your own. Just notice what you feel. You'll find that you can be aware of your own feelings without going into a reactive or control mode. This is a great practice to help you navigate issues and challenges in your intimate relationships.

Happy: When did you feel happy today?

Sad: When did you feel sad today?

Anger: When did you feel angry most recently? What was the underlying fear or hurt behind the anger?

Fear: When did you feel fearful today? What were you afraid of or anxious about?

Peace and well-being practices

Cultivate mental and emotional balance by practicing one or a combination of these ancient peace and well-being practices: yoga, meditation, chi gung, t'ai chi. You might choose a well-being practice that you know and love already or one that is new to you. If you have a practice that works well for you already, focus on your commitment and consistency in giving yourself the blessings of the practice. If you are inexperienced or new to the practice you choose, commit to doing it with a teacher, in a class or by following a book or recording. Notice the difference your peace and well-being practice makes in the moment, throughout your day and over time.

A mind vacation or day of silence

Give your mind a vacation by taking a break from the daily news, internet browsing, checking your phone except as absolutely necessary, reading, watching TV, mental stimulants like coffee, caffeinated tea or maté, or any of the other mentally driven and information gathering activities in your life. Instead, allow your mind to enjoy some silence, enjoy a sunset or beautiful view, meditate, or do something physical, simply breathe and feel, lie on the earth and let the sun shine on you. Do this for a day or more. If this sounds like torture,

Discover the activities that bring you joy and aliveness, and do them often.

or seems radical to you, start with a shorter amount of time and experience a taste of being in relationship with yourself. You might also consider finding a teacher or guide to assist you in becoming more comfortable being present, allowing and embracing of yourself. You could choose to give yourself the blessings of a retreat. Many organized retreats are offered with experienced facilitators to guide you. Or you can create one on your own.

Connecting in nature

Nature has a beautiful way of replenishing us deeply. Nature is a glorious expression of love energy. Take some time in nature and receive some of that love. This could be as simple as sitting with a tree or plant or finding a special spot from which to watch a sunrise or sunset. Choose your favorite way of being in nature or explore new ones. For me, being near moving water, ideally a clean river or ocean where I can swim, and gardening or wild-crafting are three of my favorite ways of being in nature.

Creative expression

Creative expression nourishes our sense of self and our connection with the world. It also allows us to be the contribution we are, fulfilling one of our deepest longings as human beings. As many forms of creative expression exist as there are unique spirits desiring to be expressed. Your creative expression may come forth in a classic artistic way (moving, dancing, painting, drawing, writing, making music) or it may show up in your garden or in the kitchen or in your work, or it may be something completely unique to you. Choose something that feels like play, the kind of play in which you have so much fun that you enter a time- less zone without agendas or outcomes. This is just for you! And just for fun! The most important thing about including creative expression in your daily life is that it makes you come alive. So, discover the activities that bring you joy and aliveness, and do them often to feel the exhilaration of touching this world in the way that only you can. As a bonus, you'll be pleased and surprised by the miracles this will create in your love life.

Self love and nurturing
Loving yourself the way you desire to be loved sets the ener- getic tone or vibration.

Treat yourself to:
> ~ a comfortable home & furniture

> ~ aesthetic beauty and pleasing environments

> ~ yummy sensual clothes and bedding

> ~ supportive sensual self care – massage, hot tubs, mineral baths, physical activities in which you connect with your body and senses such as enjoying dance or swimming or yoga, and being connected in nature

Our sensuality connects us with each other and the world. Our spirits rejoice and are expressed in life by virtue of receiving and manifesting through our senses. It is through this gift of sensuality, via tastes, sounds, smells, visions, and feelings, that your world comes alive. As you fully receive this blessing, you embrace being and feeling loved. Treat yourself to sensual yumminess. Go for quality, comfort, beauty and health, consciously choosing care for your body and being in each precious moment of life. Savoring the delicious moments on your own, and with your Love, welcomes and inspires being and feeling ever more love and aliveness.

How does it get any better than that?

Questions to ask:

Asking questions takes us beyond our limiting thought patterns and opens us to new possibilities and solutions. No need to know or find the answers. Simply choose or create a question that invites a positive shift or awareness. Ask the question with curiosity, speaking out loud if possible, and then release it. Be open and stay tuned to what shows up. It may manifest as a thought, a symbol, a shift or an unexpected blessing. Asking opens the door to miracles.

What choice can I make in this moment to nourish and love myself?

How can I love and embrace all of my feelings?

How can I be even more aware of the guidance and messages my feelings give to me?

What can I do or shift to tune in and listen to my body even more?

What commitments can I make now to honor the relationship I desire and choose to create?

How can I be even more committed to my own joy and well-being right now?

What if I choose to love me the way I most want to be loved?

Tools and practices to use:

1) Waterfall of Love Centering

Note: You may want to record this guided centering for yourself or you can find a link at the back of this book to my audio version, available as a download.

Find yourself a comfortable seat, either on the edge of a chair or on a cushion on the floor. Sit up tall with your spine elongated and your shoulders back and aligned over your hips. Bring your shoulders up toward your ears and back to lengthen the sides of your body and open your heart, opening your heart especially toward yourself with love and kindness. Take this time for you, giving yourself your own full attention. At first, simply taking a moment to check in with yourself to notice how you are feeling right now, physically, emotionally and energetically, without judging or needing to change anything – just noticing. (pause) Now, bring your awareness to your breath. Aware of the inhale, aware of the exhale, allowing your breath to bring you home to yourself again and again. (pause) Aware of the inhale, aware of the exhale, coming home to yourself. Now allow your awareness to drop into your heart center, tapping in to your own wellspring of love, allowing it to bubble up and fill your heart full to overflowing with love. (pause) Now tune in to the mother earth, and connect with her in whatever way works for you, knowing that she is supporting you always and receiving her love into your heart as well. (pause) Last but not least, tapping in to the love and support of the Universe, surrounding and including you, knowing that the Universe says "Yes!" to all that you truly desire and are willing to receive, receiving this universal love and support into your heart. So your heart is full and overflowing like a waterfall of love. Let this love nourish every cell of your body, nourishing your whole being. And as you're ready, bring your awareness back to your breath, aware of the inhale, aware of the exhale, staying connected with you and the love flowing within and through you as you move through your day or surrender to sleep.

2) Getting to Know Your Feelings Practice.
Create time in each day to breathe, feel and check in with yourself. Commit to setting aside 5- 15 minutes for this feeling practice. Allow yourself to sit comfortably in stillness. You might wish to rest one hand on your heart and one on your belly, or you could simply rest your hands in your lap. Allow yourself to drop in by deepening your breath, becoming aware of the breath as it flows in and out. Begin to scan your body, starting at your toes and moving up toward your head, slowly, to notice how each and every part of your body feels. You may notice places that feel tired or energized, empty or full, or tingly or yummy or achy. Notice where you feel at ease in your body and where you feel tension or discomfort and anything else you feel. Now choose a place in your body to focus on. Choose an area that is easier for you to tune into. This is likely to be one with more noticeable sensations or as I usually say, "a place in your body that is speaking more loudly." Give it your best, most loving awareness and attention, the kind of

continued...

Tools and practices to use continued

attention you might give a child who needs some TLC. Be curious and loving toward it. How does it feel? How big is the area of sensation? What emotions do you feel as you breathe into it? Give your love to all the feelings and love yourself as you feel them.

3) Befriending Your Feelings Practice.
You can do this as a practice of connecting with yourself, and as a way of connecting and sharing with your partner as well. Below you will see the four most basic feelings that we cycle through in our human moments: happy, sad, angry and fearful. By learning to recognize, befriend and express these four feelings, we enhance our capacity for navigating our own emotions and those felt by loved ones. Most of us have feelings we are in touch with, the ones that are easy or acceptable to us, and others we suppress or submerge because we judge them or find them uncomfortable to be with. Some of us commonly go to anger and avoid the feelings of fear or sadness beneath the anger, while others go to sadness and avoid anger. In this practice you'll get to cultivate a greater awareness of your feelings so you can receive the gifts and guidance they offer.

Visit with each feeling by asking and answering the questions associated with it. Answer each question with one, simple sentence. Leave out the story, explanations or reasons, and just get in touch with the feeling as you speak or write the answer. Here's an example: "I felt fearful about telling my friend that the rear view mirror of his car broke off when I adjusted it today. I was afraid he would be angry at me for breaking it." You can write your answers on a sheet of paper, or in your journal or share it with your partner or a friend with whom you've agreed to practice. Notice where and how you feel each feeling in your body. If you do this practice with someone else, it is best, at first, to get used to sharing feelings around situations that don't involve your practice partner. As you gain comfort with simply sharing and listening to each other's feelings, then you can advance to doing so even when the feelings being shared are related to each other. You will know you are ready for this more advanced version when you are able to allow each other to have any feeling. You may still have feelings of your own without going into a reactive or control mode. This is a great practice to help you navigate issues and challenges in your intimate relationships.

Happy: When did you feel happy today?

Sad: When did you feel sad today?

Anger: When did you feel angry most recently? What was the underlying fear or hurt behind the anger?

Fear: When did you feel fearful today? What were you afraid of or anxious about?

continued...

Tools and practices to use continued

4) Happiness Tool

Do something that you know brings you joy and aliveness. It may be taking time in nature. It may be to move your body in some way. It may be to do something creative that allows you to express yourself. These three examples commonly take most people to a greater level of joy. Do what calls to you.

5) Peaceful Moments Breathing Practice

This is a calming and balancing practice. Find yourself a comfortable seat, either on the edge of a chair or on a cushion on the floor. Sit up tall with your spine elongated and your shoulders back and aligned over your hips. Now bring your awareness to your breath. Aware of the inhale, aware of the exhale, allowing your breath to deepen. Begin breathing into your belly so that your belly expands like a balloon as you inhale. Pause at the top of the inhale and begin to soften your belly, allowing that softening to initiate the exhale. Let the breath become long, slow and balanced. Continue breathing like this, allowing the inhale and exhale to balance so that your breath flows in as slowly as it flows out. Enjoy the peaceful moments and take the calming effects with you into your day or night.

6) Sensual self care and love focused on your very loyal and deserving feet

Foot baths and foot rubs are some of my favorite ways to give myself and my feet some good loving. I also created a feet loving yoga sequence and we'll save that for another time. Our feet are generally overworked and under appreciated so when you bless yourself with this super yummy sensual treat, you'll also reap the added rewards of happier, healthier feet. Basic instructions: Find a tub or basin big enough for both of your feet to rest in and be submerged in warm water. Have a towel ready to dry your feet at the end. Fill the container with just enough warm water to cover your feet. You'll want the water to be as warm as you can enjoy so that it stays warm enough for long enough. Be sure to test the temperature so that you don't scald yourself. Scalding is known to occur at 120 degrees Fahrenheit and 48 degrees Celsius so your water temperature definitely needs to be less than that. I usually add some baths salts with yummy essential oils or you can simply use Epsom salts. And you might explore using bath oils or bubble bath instead. Once your foot bath is all ready and inviting, sit down and settle in for some deep relaxation. Let your feet soak until they begin to feel soft and relaxed. Then you can either use some body scrub or massage oil on one foot at a time, scrubbing and massaging in whatever ways feel most yummy for you, or you can just relax into the soaking. When you're done be sure to dry your feet gently, lovingly, and thoroughly. As an alternative you can skip the foot bath and go straight for a foot rub with your favorite massage oil, coconut oil or you can even use moisturizing

continued...

Tools and practices to use continued

lotion if that's what you have. Place a towel under your feet during the massage so that you don't end up with oil staining upholstery or dripping where you don't want it. And do dry the oil off the bottoms of your feet before you walk around so they're not slippery on the floor. Whatever you choose, allow yourself to luxuriate in your own sensuality and get to know how much pleasure you can discover through giving yourself your own loving attention.

7) Gratitude Practice:

This is one of my most powerful practices. It is one of the quickest ways I know to uplift my spirits and shift into the high state of love, joy and peace. And it is very simple. Focus your attention on the things you are grateful for in your life. Give thanks for specific things you enjoy or feel blessed by in life, one by one. You can start by writing a list of at least 99 things for which you feel grateful. Then you might choose to do this practice every evening before bed, speaking or writing your gratitude and appreciation for at least five things from the day. You could also share your gratitude practice with your partner or a friend each day. And simply take a moment of gratitude anytime you think of it and make a point to do it anytime you need an uplifting shift. After years of doing this, my practice of gratitude flows naturally throughout my every day. I often do my Gratitude Practice out loud when I'm driving alone and by the time I arrive wherever I'm going I'm in such a state of love and happiness that everyone is delighted to see me.

Actions to choose:

This is simply a list of actions based on this chapter that you might choose to take on your proactive path. I offer them as options to support you in bringing the material from this manual to life. You may choose one or more from this list or you may find something else from the chapter that inspires your action. The practices work miracles when practiced! And to enjoy the shifts and miracles, you'll need to take actions!

Action 1: Choose a tool or practice from this chapter to apply in your daily life. Choose one that resonates with you, as a starting point. Once you practice, explore and integrate that first one, then you might add another one, and so on.

Action 2: Choose just a few questions to ask from the lists at the end of this chapter to write on sticky notes and post them in places where you'll see them often. Each time you see one of your posted questions, pause and ask it out loud if possible, or silently if necessary. Remember to breathe and allow the question to resonate for a moment.

Action 3: Take some time in nature. This could be as simple as sitting with a tree or plant or finding a special spot from which to watch a sunrise or sunset. Choose your favorite way of being in nature or explore new ones.

continued...

Actions to choose *continued*

Action 4: Do something to express your creative self. Your creative expression may come forth in a classic artistic way (moving, dancing, painting, drawing, writing, making music . . .) or you might express it in your garden or in the kitchen or in your work, or it may be something completely unique to you. Choose something that feels like play, the kind of play in which you have so much fun that you enter a timeless zone without agendas or outcomes. This is just for you! And just for fun! The most important thing about including creative expression in your daily life is that it makes you come alive. So, choose something that brings you joy and aliveness.

Bonus action: Write to me with your love miracles and I will celebrate each and every one! You will also be contributing to our love evolution movement by creating an expanding culture of healthy, thriving relationships in the world. I am exhilarated and motivated by your love miracle stories and the extraordinary results that unfold when you implement these simple yet powerful practices into your life.

Celebrations!

Celebrate every time you make a shift, have a new awareness or insight, make a new choice, take an action in alignment with what you desire or experience a miracle. Celebrations can be as simple as pausing to acknowledge a shift with a deep breath and a smile, a dance of joy, a hoot and a holler, sharing your success with a loved one or anything else that feels fun and acknowledges the shifts and miracles taking place, whether small or huge.

6

Choosing and Receiving the Love You Desire

*Clear Your Past, Clarify Your Desires
and Get Ready to Embrace
Your New Love.*

Opening to new love

CREATE SPACE IN YOUR HOME, YOUR HEART AND YOUR
life to receive your new Love. This is the first step to let your
whole self and the Universe know you are ready.

Creating space in your home to receive your new Love

If you start with creating space on a physical level in your home, it can clear and move the energy so that all the other steps flow more easily.

Here's an example of how this worked for a dear friend of mine who really wanted a life partner.

My friend shared with me how discouraged he was feeling with dating. He described the frustrating pattern he was experiencing. It went like this. He would meet a woman, she would seem interested and things would seem as if they were progressing toward a relationship. Then he'd invite her to his home and things would fall flat.

Now, I had been to his home and I knew that it would need a few changes to be welcoming to the women he was naturally inclined to attract. I asked him if he was open to a few suggestions that would probably make a big difference. He was open, so I gave him a small list of things to change. Though he was quite surprised by the things I suggested, he was so committed to having a life partner that he made all the changes immediately. A few weeks later he called to tell me how well this had worked, that he had met a special woman, had invited her to his home and she was still interested. It seemed quite promising and turned into wedding bells within the year. Last time I spoke to him they were still happily married.

Now, not everyone has such instant results. My friend was clearly ready on all levels to the point at which he had no resistance at all to making changes to his home in order to welcome his Love with open arms. His bachelor home had actually been pushing women away at an unconscious level, so with a few simple changes that would never have occurred to him, it was easy for him to have rapid and delightful results.

Your turn. Are you ready? Here are some basic guidelines to make this shift. Especially if you've been living a single lifestyle, you'll need to shift your thinking and approach and start including and welcoming another being into your world and day-to-day moments.

Create space in your home, your heart and your life to receive your new Love.

Your first step is to take a look at your living space. Imagine your Love is there with you. What needs to change to make the space more welcoming and inclusive for your Love? Here are some of the most basic things that create an intentional space for coupling.

> ~ Do you have a place where the two of you can comfortably eat together and share connection?
> ~ Do you have pairs of plates, glasses, and utensils?
> ~ Is there a cozy place to sit and visit?
> ~ Is there room in your bed and are both sides of the bed accessible?
> ~ Is the bed an appropriate love nest for the one you desire to attract?
> ~ Is there a nightstand on both sides?
> ~ Is there a place for your Love to hang some clothes?
> ~ Is there a place in your bathroom for an extra bath towel?

Think about the person you're calling in. What else do you notice that might need some adjustment for the one you're calling in to feel at home? Or, if you are in a relationship that you would like to take to a long-term commitment, here's a question you can ask that will show you and your chosen one whether you are really ready for commitment. How could I make my home more comfortable and welcoming for you? Be curious and open as you listen to understand whatever is shared. Ask encouraging and clarifying questions. And also notice what feelings you have. This is a sweet exploration and a great opportunity for deepening into intimacy.

Creating space in your heart to receive your new Love

Clear your past, clear your wounds, fears and limiting beliefs and cultivate a fabulously fun relationship with yourself to be fully ready for new love. This may seem like a big hurdle if you are not accustomed to this kind of inner work. It doesn't have to be a long, drawn out and arduous process. It can be quick, sometimes easy and will almost certainly be extremely liberating. Doing your inner work first will actually save you a lot of time, suffering and heartache. So, if you have not healed from past relationships, including your family relationships, find a qualified facilitator or coach to help you with this important clearing process. Explore, excavate and clear the limiting beliefs you've picked up or conclusions you've drawn along your journey about love, intimacy, sex and relationship.

Lastly, if you have any unfinished business or loose ends in your life, do what it takes to come to resolution or completion. Unfinished business takes energy from anything new you desire to create, so completing any loose ends will open doors in other areas of your life—like career, health and finances, in addition to making space for your relationship.

Creating space in your life to receive your new Love

Look at the pattern or schedule of your day-to-day life. Again, if you've been living a single lifestyle, you'll need to shift your thinking and approach to start including and welcoming another being into your world and daily moments. Do your days and weeks have the flexibility to include connection time with your Love? If not, what would you be willing to shift or let go of to create space for a relationship? Begin making space for the kinds of activities you'd like to share with your partner. Start including these things in your days. Take time to enjoy your own company in the way you would share yourself with your Love. For example, if you like to dance, turn on some music and take time to dance in your living room, go out dancing or take some dance classes on your own or with a friend. If you like to share time in nature, go to some places you would like to take your partner. Don't wait to enjoy life once your partner arrives. Live fully now and your Love will be drawn to you like a magnet!

Placing your order with the Universe

OK, this part is really fun! You've done your clearing, you're having a great time, enjoying your own company and you're including more of the fun you want to share in your life. *Now you're ready* for the relationship of your dreams.

Maybe you've had a relationship like this before, or maybe you know a couple who have this kind of relationship. Maybe you've always known that someday you would have the kind of love you truly desire and are meant to have. Or maybe you've just imagined it and hope that it can be realized. Take some time, right now, to write down all the vital qualities of the relationship of your dreams, becoming even more clear and specific about the essentials of this amazing relationship. This is especially important if you've had a tendency to

The Universe says "Yes!" when you place your request and you are willing to receive.

attract and create relationships that don't match what you truly desire, because you will likely repeat the picture you hold in your mind until you change that picture. You get to start over and revise your vision right now!

This is like placing your order with the Universe from the menu of infinite possibilities. In my experience, the Universe is very literal and will give us *exactly* what we ask for. (Perhaps you've heard the old adage, "Be careful what you ask for.") What you leave out may be left out and what you include will likely show up.

Here's one example:

I once placed a request with the Universe and left out some of my most essential relationship qualities. I was so used to being seen, held and adored in my relationships that I completely forgot to specify these elements in the new relationship I was requesting. So the beautiful man that showed up had most of the qualities I desired yet was quite unable to see me, adore me and hold safe intimate space for my vulnerabilities, growth and evolution. At the time he was going through a powerful personal transformation himself and was attracted to me for the space I could hold. When it quickly became clear to me that this imbalance in our relationship was not about to change, I opted out. And back to the drawing board I went! Revisiting my request, which I had put in writing for extra potency, I laughed when I realized that I had indeed received what I asked for.

So, it's worth being careful to place a request that will totally please you when it arrives. The Universe says "Yes!" when you place your request and you are willing to receive.

Aligning with new love

Now, allow yourself to align with this vision. Be the One who is ready to receive the phenomenal relationship you just requested from the Universe. Like attracts like, so if you want your partner to show up in all those delightful ways, connect with you and stay for a while, then you need show up too! You already know the person you imagine you'll be when your partner is in your life. Be that person, *now*!

OK...you've created and aligned with your vision, and you're ready to receive the sweet love you've envisioned. Energize it even more by imagining yourself living in this vision until it becomes real for you. Tune in to how you feel as you live it, noticing with all your senses the smells, tastes, sounds, sights and feelings in your body and emotions. The smells are especially helpful in making it very real. Let it become more and more vivid and alive for you, and when it feels real, that's when your love miracle will begin to unfold, naturally and magically.

Making conscious choices in alignment with your highest unfolding

If you have had unhealthy relationships in the past, especially if your last relationship was an unhappy situation for you, it is especially important to tune into choosing consciously rather than falling desperately or romantically into your next relationship. Give yourself permission to choose and embrace your new Love!

When you choose your relationships consciously and intentionally, the quality of your relationships will improve dramatically. Most of the time, when people say they have a "bad or broken picker," what is really going on is that they are just choosing unconsciously even though they actually *do* have an intuitive awareness of the warning signs or red flags. In reality, they are ignoring the awareness of what they already know and sense in the bigger picture, and instead, are following the excitement and attraction to some *part* of what they desire, whether it be physical attraction or companionship or financial stability or sharing some fun activities. And to this they add a big dose of denial or wishing and hoping that those other things will change for the better. This fantasy of love is a high-drama path to disappointment or disaster. Unfortunately, it is more common in our modern culture than the healthy version of consciously and intentionally making choices that are in alignment with our own clarity of the love and relationship we truly desire. This is precisely why it is helpful to first become really clear and place your order with the Universe. You will need to hold that expanded vision when you're tempted to jump at a partial platter rather than the whole thing—that might have you preoccupied when the full platter of your dream relationship is about to be served.

Here are some tools to use and questions to ask yourself that will assist you in choosing consciously in alignment with your inner wisdom and guidance regarding a relationship you are considering. You can do this as you are connecting with someone you are attracted to. Or, if that's too much of a challenge, then do this by yourself just after parting from a connection with that one you are considering, while the experience is still very fresh for you.

Choosing your partner by listening to your inner guidance

~ First, tune in to your body and notice what you are feeling physically and emotionally.

~ Now expand your awareness to include more time and space and tune into the bigger picture. You will probably already have a lot of clarity at this point and you may already have an obvious choice.

~ Now tune in to the energy of your connection while opening yourself to receive a full sense of all of what's there.

~ Ask: "What is my intuition or gut feeling about moving forward with this relationship?

~ If I trust and listen to my intuition, what will I choose?

~ If I choose this relationship, will it inspire, energize and bring out the best in me? If I choose this relationship will it drain, deplete or hold me back from my highest expression?"

~ Now trust the intuitive, energetic, higher guidance responses you receive.

Warning: As tempting as it may be, do not use your logical mind to "figure this out." This is one of the biggest mistakes people make, and it's because you can talk yourself into or out of anything and your unconscious beliefs and programming will be in charge of that decision. Our inner guidance system works really well for choosing relationships when we are listening. In talking with those who have had relationships that were not a good match and destined to fail, it is common for them to say that they were aware of the red flags early on, but didn't pay attention. So you can change that simply by paying attention and listening to your full awareness.

Practice cultivating healthy relationships.

As I mentioned in the introduction, the tools and practices in this book can be applied in all your relationships. So I invite you to practice them with your family and friends, at home, at work and in all your social interactions. This will deepen and enrich the relationships you already have in your life, while bringing you into alignment with the qualities you desire in your new love relationship. If you are single and dating, focus on cultivating friendships with people who share the qualities you admire and appreciate, who inspire you to be your best self. Take time to develop nourishing friendships.

In our culture, we have a romantic notion of being "swept off our feet" or "falling in love." Doesn't this sound somewhat unstable to you and maybe even indicative of self-abandonment? Let yourself be curious about this. Have you ever really listened to most "love" songs and thought about the literal meaning of the words? Many lyrics suggest that love is as dramatic as a heart attack and the romanticized, often superficial, dynamics don't seem very desirable, healthy or fun. Often the words describe a detrimentally unhealthy relationship with a lack of boundaries, a loss of self or toxic elements of judgment and blame. Full awareness and conscious choice are often missing.

If you find yourself wanting to rush into romance, check in with yourself to see what's creating the urgency for you. What's really going on for you? Slow down and listen to your inner guidance.

Also, be aware of using sex as a way to instantly fill a longing and create a sense of the closeness you desire. This will backfire if the foundational roots of real intimacy are missing. I know this may sound less than romantic. However, I can tell you from personal experience that starting with a truly caring friendship that unfolded into deep and genuine love has taken me into the sweetest, most heart opening intimacy and unwavering love of my life.

When friendship unfolds into genuine love and a relationship ripens into the courtship phase of coupling, this too is worth savoring. Allow yourself to enjoy and luxuriate in this sweet journey on your path to love.

Questions to ask:

Asking questions opens us to new possibilities and solutions. No need to know or find the answers. Let the answers come to you. Just ask the question with a sense of curiosity, speaking out loud if possible, and then release it. An answer may come instantly or later. It may come in thoughts, words or as guidance in another form. Be open and stay tuned. Asking opens the door to miracles.

How can I be even more open to new love right now?

What can I shift now to invite and welcome the relationship I truly desire and choose to create?

How can I make my home more welcoming and inclusive for my new Love?

What action steps can I take to move towards the love, happiness and amazing relationship I am meant to share?

What do I want to celebrate about how I relate to myself?

How can I create space in my week to do an activity I'd enjoy sharing with my partner? How can I be even more committed to my own happiness and readiness?

What qualities are vital to my amazing relationship?

What choices can I make today to nourish healthy relationships in my life?

How will our relationship be different if we focus on the quality of our friendship first?

What fears, wounds, limiting beliefs or unfinished business do I need to attend to?

continued...

Questions to ask continued

What will be the most effective and easiest way for me to create space in my heart and my life to receive my new Love?

How much more fun can we share in love if we begin by proactively choosing and committing to happily ever after as our path?

If I choose and receive the love I truly desire, what difference might that make for our children, our community and future generations?

Tools and practices to use:

1) Creating space in your home to receive your new Love If you start with creating space on a physical level in your home, it can clear the way for all the other steps to flow more easily. This tool works on both a practical as well as energetic levels.

Take a fresh look at your living space. Imagine yourself as your new Love entering your home for the first time. Walk through your home with an eye for how you two might share the space together. How welcoming does it feel? How comfortable is it for sharing? What would make the space even more welcoming, inclusive and comfortable?

Here is a checklist you can use to create an intentional coupling energy in your home:

Is there a cozy place to sit and visit?

Do you have a place where the two of you can comfortably eat & connect together?

Do you have pairs of plates, glasses, and utensils?

Is there space to share your favorite home activities (yoga, dancing, movies)?

Is there room in your bed and are both sides of the bed accessible?

Is the bed an appropriate love nest for the one you desire to attract?

Is there a nightstand on both sides?

Is there a place for your Love to hang some clothes?

Is there a place in your bathroom for an extra bath towel?

What else do you notice that might need some adjustment for the One you're calling in to feel at home?

2) Living fully alive and celebrating life

Take time to enjoy your own company in ways you would also enjoy sharing with your Love. For example, if you like to dance, turn on some music and take time to dance in your living room, go out dancing or take some dance classes. If you like to share time in nature, take yourself to some places you'd take your partner. Don't wait to enjoy life once your partner arrives. Live fully now and your Love will be drawn to you like a magnet!

continued...

Tools and practices to use *continued*

3) Calling in your new Love

Take some time to write down all the vital qualities of the relationship of your dreams, becoming even more clear and specific about the essentials of this amazing relationship. Formulate this into the form of a written request to place with the Universe. Then speak your request out loud and place your written version in a special place. If you enjoy ceremonies and rituals, you could turn this into a potent one. Do whatever feels sacred and powerful to you. You can use this practice to place requests with the Universe for other aspects of your life too.

Actions to choose:

This is simply a list of actions based on this chapter that you might choose to take on your proactive path. I offer them as options to support you in bringing the material from this manual to life. You may choose one or more from this list or you may find something else from the chapter that inspires your action. The practices work miracles when practiced! And to enjoy the shifts and miracles, you'll need to take actions!

Action 1: Choose a tool or practice from this chapter to apply in your daily life. Choose one that resonates with you, as a starting point. Once you practice, explore and integrate that first one, then you might add another one, and so on.

Action 2: Choose just a few questions from the "Questions to ask" section of this chapter. Choose the ones that inspire you. Write each question on a sticky note and post them in places where you'll see them often. When you see a question, pause and ask it. Remember to breathe and allow the question to resonate for a moment. Keep asking and stay open for guidance, awareness and miracles.

Action 3: Find a qualified facilitator or coach to help you clear your past, clear your wounds, fears and limiting beliefs and cultivate a fabulously fun relationship with yourself to be fully ready for new love.

Action 4: Complete any unfinished business and tie any loose ends in your life to open your flow of energy. This will also remove nagging distractions, allowing you to fully focus on creating the amazing relationship you are meant to share.

Action 5: If you are currently dating, use the "Choosing your partner by listening to your inner guidance" tools and questions from this chapter to make conscious choices in alignment with your highest unfolding.

Bonus action: Write to me with your love miracles and I will celebrate each and every one! You will also be contributing to our love evolution movement by creating an expanding culture of healthy, thriving relationships in the world. I am exhilarated and motivated by your love miracle stories and the extraordinary results that unfold when you implement these simple yet powerful practices into your life.

Celebrations!

Celebrate every time you make a shift, have a new awareness or insight, make a new choice, take an action in
alignment with what you desire or experience a miracle.
Celebrations can be as simple as pausing to acknowledge
a shift with a deep breath and a smile, a dance of joy, a
hoot and a holler, sharing your success with a loved one
or anything else that feels fun and acknowledges the
shifts and miracles taking place, whether small or huge.

7

For Women: The Secrets to Being Deliciously Adored

Six CHARMS to Produce Delicious Results in Your Relationships & Your Life!

WHAT IF YOU COULD RELEASE WHATEVER IT IS THAT KEEPS you from being completely and deliciously adored, and open yourself up to miracles and sweet surprises that show up in your relationships and your life?

What if you could do that with total ease?

Welcome to the secrets of being—and feeling—deliciously adored! Since you are here now reading this book, I know you are on track for having the relationships and the life you would actually love to have. Being adored by others follows naturally once you take the first essential step of loving and adoring yourself, as you've just read in "Chapter 5: Your First Love is You." It is elucidated even further in the secrets I'm about to share with you.

Let me begin with a little story of what led me to uncover these secrets—aka "The Six CHARMS to Being Deliciously Adored."

I discovered the need to share my experience on this topic of being adored after years of hearing comments from people such as: "*Everyone* is in love with *you*." or "Oh, of course anyone would do that for *you*!" And then another comment I've heard from quite a few women: "I don't find sweet little surprises on *my* doorstep." This last one surprised me. "Really"? I asked, and the replies baffled me enough to ask more questions. Being and feeling adored is something so natural to me that it seemed puzzling to find that, even though some women feel this way, many women do not. I wondered: What is it that I'm being or doing that's different . . . the difference that if I could know it and share it, would allow all women to be able to feel adored? The insights that came to me next were so much fun that I immediately turned them into a seminar for women called "Being Your Naturally Irresistible and Loveable Self," which proved to be a real hit. This chapter is based on the insights I shared in that seminar.

Let me roll out the red carpet for you here to receive the secrets that have naturally attracted to me the kindest, most adoring friends and partners anyone could ever ask for. And you'll be able to use these same secrets to create the adoring relationships you truly desire. So, don't just believe what I say. And do use these secrets with wild abandon to discover for yourself what else is possible. Use these secrets if, and only if, you are willing to have lots of delightful new options and sweet surprises. I promise you

What if you are naturally, irresistibly attractive and loveable simply by being you?

that if you don't use these tools they will do nothing for you, and if you do use them with wild abandon, delicious miracles will unfold.

I can hardly wait to hear what unfolds for you!

What if you are naturally, irresistibly attractive and loveable simply by being you? What if you have never been anything but naturally loveable and irresistible? And what if the only things that keep you from being as fully loved and adored as you desire, are the ways in which you don't allow yourself to receive? In short, that means to receive attention, to receive joy and pleasure, to receive and express all of you, to receive being fully seen.

What would it be like to be you and to be seen, loved and adored?

I don't promise that all of what unfolds will be comfortable for you. Change isn't always comfortable. And if you are willing to be with the discomfort, it will also change … and in the process you will open the gates to more love and sweetness in your relationships and in your life.

The 6 CHARMS to Being Deliciously Adored

Confidence
Happiness
Adoration
Romance
Meaning
Sensuality

Confidence

Embrace yourself with total allowance and acknowledgement.
> ~ Dress for your own comfort & enjoyment to honor & please yourself.
> ~ Ask yourself empowering and uplifting questions.

Exude warmth, ease & natural radiance—smiling allows your nervous system to know you're OK, and allows others to know you're open and receptive.

Recognize & trust the support of the Universe.

Confidence starts with being naturally you. You can't get to true confidence by trying to be anything or anyone else. And confidence can be quiet, too. It all lies in how you hold yourself and feel about yourself. Sometimes quiet confidence can be even more powerful because it doesn't need to prove anything. The more you come into completely accepting, allowing and embracing yourself, the more confidence will become your natural state. The better you feel, the easier this is. So, loving, accepting and acknowledging yourself in the way you desire to be loved, accepted and acknowledged is a great way to feel good and build confidence.

Celebration is one of my favorite practices because it combines the energies of acknowledgment and gratitude. Whenever I introduce celebrations to my clients, I notice that it accelerates their progress. Do this practice at least once each day. I encourage you to do this practice any time you're inspired and before bed each night to set the tone for your next day.

Here's the practice:

Speak out loud and/or write in your journal at least three to five things you are celebrating or acknowledging yourself for that occurred in the past 24-48 hours. You can include a way you were being, accomplishments or goals you achieved, insights or awareness you had, practices you implemented, a shift you had or an action you took. You might celebrate ways you've touched others or expressed kindness. You can appreciate and celebrate ways in which you honored your values, such as honesty or integrity or authenticity or growth and evolution. You might remember and acknowledge a specific time when you expressed a special quality, talent or gift you have. Celebrate little things as well as big things. Make this a practice in your life and it will definitely contribute to your feeling confident, magnificent and joyful!

Another way to embrace yourself and inspire your confidence is to dress in ways that are comfortable and yummy for you. In fact, this is so energetically potent that I invite you to go through your clothes closets, drawers and shelves and get rid of absolutely everything that doesn't give you a resounding YES! If you only feel OK in it, then it goes. This may dramatically reduce your wardrobe, which is perfect because now you know that anything you pull out to wear is going to feel awesome! I know this might be a leap for you . . . so you can do this incrementally by putting all those "to go" items in bags or boxes and keeping them in storage for three to six months before you actually get rid of them. This way you can do the experiment and experience the invigorating shift it makes before you fully commit, and if it turns out there is anything you really want to keep, you'll be able to pull it out before the final release.

The other part to this wardrobe shift is to only buy clothes that have that same resounding YES! energy. I promise this is a radical "feel magnificent move" because it shifts so many unconscious limiting beliefs and energetic drains in the process.

Being adored by others follows naturally once you take the first essential step of loving and adoring yourself.

Would you like one more confidence booster? This is a fun one and opens the gates into the realm of miracles. What if you knew without a doubt that the Universe has got your back? What miracles would you have access to if you realized and trusted that the Universe is saying Yes! to your every wish and desire? How much confidence would you have knowing that you've got the Universe on your side?

We have learned scientifically through quantum physics that whatever we think actually becomes. We now know that the Universe, or creation, is constantly responding to our thoughts to create our reality. A psychological expression of this is a self-fulfilling prophecy. When we focus on a certain outcome as being true, it then becomes true. So, how can you fully receive this support from the Universe, allowing yourself to harness this awesome creative power and confidence booster? Start by asking that question precisely: "How can I fully receive this support from the Universe?" And then follow the guidance that comes. The first thing that jumps out for me is to be even more aware of my thoughts and choose them consciously. Knowing that the Universe is responding to my thoughts, wishes and desires elevates them as *extra* worthy of my attention. One of my favorite ways to focus my thoughts and collaborate with the Universe is by asking questions that will lead where I wish to go. We can ask: "How can I focus my thoughts in alignment with what I truly desire to create?" Or, the Universe might have something even better lined up, so another question to ask might be: "What can I create that's even better than this?" I sometimes add: "Universe, please show me." You'll also find a centering practice at the end of this chapter that will allow you to tune into and expand your heart to access the abundant love and support available to you.

Happiness

Allow yourself to be pleased.
Recognize & receive love in the many ways it is given.
Invite yourself to receive even more.

> ~ Focus on what you enjoy & choose more of it.

> ~ Know, honor and express your preferences.

Allow yourself to be pleased. When your Love does something that pleases you, receive it fully by showing your pleasure, happiness and delight. You know how good it feels to give something to someone and see, hear or feel their delight when they receive it. Yes? When you receive with authentic delight, you are giving your Love the gift of feeling the pleasure of giving. If you don't allow yourself to be pleased or happy, and don't express it, eventually your partner will give up attempting to please you. This is probably the #1 Secret to being deliciously adored, and most women who don't feel adored are missing it. This means that it's important to highlight your enjoyment of what is already pleasing to you rather than to complain about what's missing. Once your partner is fully enjoying the pleasure of *you* being pleased, then, and only then, can you introduce your wish for another delightful possibility and invite it. Trust me on this one! Make this shift completely, practice it consistently and see for yourself. You'll be pleased by the results and so will your Love!

If this is a stretch for you, I invite you to explore your capacity for receiving, ideally with the expert assistance of a mentor or coach. Being a good receiver is essential to feeling adored because, no matter how much your partner loves and adores you, if you can't take it in, you won't be able to feel it. When you do your inner work to shift and clear anything that keeps you from fully receiving pleasure and delight, life becomes unbelievably sweet and delicious.

Recognizing and receiving love in the many ways it is given can transform the quality of your relationships. And it takes practice. Often we miss the love being given because it is given in a form we don't recognize.

Here's an example:
My grandmother loved offering comments to me, my sisters and my mother, about what we could do to our hairstyle that, in her *opinion, would be more flattering. She would regularly critique the hairstyles of the women she loved. Though this could be received as criticism, I chose to receive it as love. Nana would say something like, "Tracie, I like your hair when you wear it in*

this way . . . " and I'd respond with a squeeze and a smile, "Oh Nana, I know you love me and want me to look my best. Thank you for caring." Or I'd simply say, "I love you, Nana." She felt her love and comment received so she didn't need to continue the hair discussion. It was like a little love ritual. And if I had taken it as criticism, I could have felt hurt or rejected or responded harshly to her and the whole situation would have been completely different, and not nearly as sweet.

So here's the practice:

Look for the love. If you are not feeling loved and adored by your Love, pause right now and contemplate how things he does or says may be a way of expressing his love. Let yourself receive and soak in the love being expressed even if it's not the ideal way for you. It may be the way he learned to love as a child because it's the way a special person loved him, or it may be the way he most wants to be loved. Maybe this special someone feeds you, or takes care of you in practical ways, or asks questions with concern for you or challenges you to be better in some way or gives you what he considers to be good advice. Even if what he is doing or saying isn't actually helpful or in alignment with who you are, it may still be coming from a place of love.

In other chapters we look at ways to make requests so that you can also ask for love and support in the ways that work best for you. Meanwhile, this practice of being able to receive love in all its many forms expands your capacity exponentially to receive and feel love in the ways you truly desire as well.

Invite yourself to receive even more. What do you enjoy? What's fun for you? Give yourself whatever most inspires your happiness on a daily basis. Giving to yourself is a practice of receiving your own precious love. What would it be like to prioritize *you* with your time, attention and money? If you've never done so, allow yourself to find out. Loving you and enjoying life is a clear message to the Universe about what you are willing to receive. And I'm not talking about retail therapy here. Buying lots of clothes and things can be a promise or fantasy of loving yourself, and if it's an empty promise, the pleasure will be very short lived. It may likely lead to more emptiness, and often to more retail therapy. I'm talking about truly loving yourself with quality time and attention that lead to meaningful moments.

Part two of receiving more is to know and honor your own preferences, the things that please you most. When you honor your own preferences, you create space for them to be honored by others. When you share your preferences openly and honestly, it makes it easy for your partner and friends to know what pleases you and to enjoy doing that. One male friend of mine put it this way: "If we know where the bull's eye is, (i.e., what your preferences are) it is pretty easy to hit the bull's eye instead of making a shot in the dark." If you pay attention, you'll hear men express their desire to know how best to please and provide in many ways. Frequently, I've heard men use these words of willingness: "I'm trainable." What I hear in that is that these men care and want to show up in service, to please and provide for the ones they love. What an endearing and admirable quality!

Happy and Joyful Partner Exercise:
This is a fun way to get even more in touch with what brings you into a state of happiness. With a partner, take turns asking each other: "When are you happy and joyful?" Receive your partner's response by reflecting it back to him. So, if your partner says: "I'm happy and joyful when I practice yoga," you receive that by saying back to him: "You're happy and

joyful when you practice yoga." Feel free to be playful and energetically aligned as you share and reflect. Now switch. Do this at least 11 times each and keep going until you're tuning into the less obvious things you may have forgotten about. Once you're complete, you might want to make notes of any insights or reminders for yourself.

Adoration
Adore and you will be adored.
   ~ Notice and highlight adorable/admirable qualities in others.
   ~ Be like the dance partner or the complement that brings out the best in others & allows them to shine.

Being adoring is an adorable quality, for sure. Here's where we get to apply the golden rule with a slight twist. Adore those you love in the way they love to be adored. Learn your Love's pleasures and preferences. Show your partner love in the way he'll recognize most easily. Pay attention to his delight. Notice what brings him joy. Ask leading questions to gather more information and be sure to express your appreciation of him. You might find that bringing out his best qualities, the things that inspire him to feel great about himself, and highlighting those will contribute magnificently to his feelings of being adored. Allow yourself to be curious, playful and creative with all of this. Have as much fun as possible in being one who adores.

Romance
Practice old-fashioned charms.
   ~ Be well groomed and express your naturally delightful, gracious, fun, entertaining self in whatever way is authentic for you.

Show your sweet sentimental & tender self, revealing more of you to be adored.

Let romance breathe vitality and longevity into your love life.

Express your romance (love, passion, devotion, fondness, warmth, affection) *in unlimited and creative ways*—aesthetically pleasing spaces, ambiance, music, cards, poems, thoughtful gifts, food, art . . .

Romance is so much a part of our human nature, and yet within its meanings, we reveal our limiting belief that the love of our dreams is either unattainable or unlikely to last. What if we can have it all? I have noticed that couples in happy, long lasting relationships have usually sustained their romantic qualities and charms over time. This romance nourishes the sweetness, adoration and lightheartedness in their relationships and is inspiring to witness. So, if being and feeling adored appeals to you, cultivate your authentic expression of old-fashioned charms. To be fully adored, reveal your sweet sentimental and tender sides. Enrich your relationship with romantic qualities of love, passion, devotion, fondness, warmth and affection in abundant, unbridled and creative ways. Let romance breathe vitality and longevity into your love life.

Meaning
Express what is meaningful to you:
- ~ Reveal yourself. Reveal your vulnerability, your passion and your priorities.
- ~ Share your feelings, frequently, sincerely & incrementally. Share in bite-sized increments. Sprinkle. Don't dump.

~ Express what is meaningful and important for you to
share. Allow the rest to be a mystery. Does anyone else
really need to know every thought or experience or feeling you've ever had?

When you share what you hold dear, you allow your dear ones
into your inner being. You allow them to know you in your
authenticity, to relate to you, to be inspired by you and the gift
that you are, to care about you and what gives your life purpose
and meaning. You give them enough of you to adore. You also
give them enough information to know how to adore you. They
know what inspires and touches you so it becomes easier for
them to touch you. They know your priorities and purpose so it
becomes easier for them to honor and support you in your life.
They know what brings you joy so it becomes easier for them
to bring you joy. When you allow it to be easier, you naturally
receive more honoring and adoring.

By revealing your authentic you, you also attract the ones who
will adore you and screen out those who are not in alignment
with your authentic self.

Prioritize what you share with others. Choose what is most
important and meaningful to you and share *those* things. Don't
just dump your insides all over the people in your life. It would be
like having to wade through all the thoughts, *her*story and experiences of my whole entire evolution in order to find the gems that
are worth publishing in this manual. TMI, right? I am not talking
about withholding or hiding things that reveal your humanity.
Those are especially important. I am talking about the minutia
or the mind clutter and chatter that may be more of a hindrance
or distraction, rather than a contribution to really knowing you.
Let those be part of the mystery. Mystery is what balances the

sharing, and you get to choose between them before sharing. Choosing consciously makes all the difference.

Revealing your whole self also creates a safe space for your dear ones and inspires them to share authentically and meaningfully, too, enriching the quality of your relationships and the mutual adoration between you.

Sensuality

Luxuriate in life!
Enjoy your senses and share the delicious moments.
Treat yourself to:

> ~ yummy sensual clothes and bedding
>
> ~ a comfortable home & furniture
>
> ~ aesthetic beauty and pleasing environments
>
> ~ sensual self care – massage, baths, physical activities in which you connect with your body and enjoy your innately sensual being such as dancing or swimming or yoga, as well as giving yourself retreats and connection time in nature

Our sensuality connects us with each other and the world. Our spirits rejoice and are expressed in life by virtue of receiving and manifesting through our senses. It is this gift of sensuality, via tastes, sounds, smells, visuals, and feelings, that your world comes alive. As you fully receive this blessing, you embrace being adored. Treat yourself to sensual yumminess. Go for quality, comfort, beauty and health, consciously choosing care for your body and being in each precious moment of life. Savoring the delicious moments on your own, and with your Love, welcomes and inspires being and feeling ever more deliciously adored.

Questions to ask:

Asking questions opens us to new possibilities and solutions. No need to know or find the answers. Let the answers come to you. Just ask the question with a sense of curiosity, speaking out loud if possible, and then release it. An answer may come instantly or later. It may come in thoughts, words or as guidance in another form. Be open and stay tuned. Asking opens the door to miracles.

What if I could release what keeps me from being completely and deliciously adored and open myself up to miracles and sweet surprises?

What if I am naturally, irresistibly attractive and loveable simply by being me?

What if I have never been anything but naturally loveable and irresistible?

How can I receive even more joy and pleasure?

What would it be like to be to be seen, loved and adored?

How can I accept and embrace myself even more fully today?

What miracles will unfold if I choose happiness over being right and stop making me or anyone else wrong?

How can I fully receive the Universal support, allowing me to harness this creative power and confidence booster?

How can I focus my thoughts in alignment with what I truly desire to create now?

What can I create that's even better than this? Universe, please show me.

Tools and practices to use:

1) Yoga Practice
Practice yoga regularly and consistently. This practice contributes to my confidence daily and I see it change the lives of those who commit to the practice, again and again.

2) Practice Adoring
Adore those you love in the way they love to be adored. Learn your Love's pleasures and preferences. Show your partner love in the way he'll recognize most easily. Pay attention to his delight. Notice what brings him joy. Ask leading questions to gather more information and be sure to express your appreciation of him. You might find that bringing out his best qualities, the things that inspire him to feel great about himself, and highlighting those will contribute magnificently to his feelings of being adored. Allow yourself to be curious, playful and creative with all of this. Have as much fun as possible in being one who adores.

Actions to choose:

This is simply a list of actions based on this chapter that you might choose to take on your proactive path. I offer them as options to support you in bringing the material from this manual to life. You may choose one or more from this list or you may find something else from the chapter that inspires your action. The practices work miracles when practiced! And to enjoy the shifts and miracles, you'll need to take actions!

Action 1: Read and take actions from the list of possibilities in "Chapter 5: Your First Love is You." How many ways can you discover in which to feel exhilarated and joyful, to love and embrace yourself and to be even happier than ever before?

continued...

Actions to choose *continued*

Action 2: Write a list of 99 appreciations and acknowl-edgements of yourself. You can appreciate qualities, talents or gifts you have or, even better, you can get specific and remember a time when you expressed the quality, talent or gift. You can include accomplishments or goals achieved. You can list ways you've touched others or expressed kindness. You might appreciate ways in which you honor your values, such as honesty or integrity or authenticity or growth and evolution. Writing this list may stretch you a little bit, or a big bit, and it may take a few days to make the whole list. Stick with it. You are building your muscles of appreciation and self-confidence and both of these muscles need to be strengthened to expand your capacity for adoring connections. Expressing appreciation is one of the most effective ways to deepen our human connection because, when we appreciate someone, we allow them to feel seen. And practicing this with yourself is a splendid place to begin.

Action 3: Give some time and focus to develop mastery with something new that inspires you. This could be a physical capacity like skiing or dancing, improving your intuition, or refining a skill like playing a musical instru-ment or speaking a language.

Action 4: Do the "Happy and Joyful Partner Exercise": This is a fun way to get even more in touch with what brings you into a state of happiness. With a partner, take turns asking each other, "When are you happy and joyful?" Receive your partner's response by reflecting it back to him. So, if your partner says, "I'm happy and joyful when I practice yoga," you receive that by saying, "You're happy and joyful when you practice yoga." Feel free to be playful and energetically aligned as you share and reflect. Now switch. Do this at least 11 times each and keep going until you're tuning into the less obvious things you may have forgotten about. Once you're complete, you might want to make notes of any insights or reminders for yourself.

Action 5: Allow yourself to luxuriate in life more. Find a way to expand or enhance your sensuality. Make it a priority to enjoy and share delicious moments. Treat yourself to some sensual self care—a massage, a bath, dancing, swimming, yoga, give yourself a retreat, or enjoy some time in nature.

Bonus action: Write to me with your love miracles and I will celebrate each and every one! You will also be contributing to our love evolution movement by creating an expanding culture of healthy, thriving relationships in the world. I am exhilarated and motivated by your love miracle stories and the extraordinary results that unfold when you implement these simple yet powerful practices into your life.

Celebrations!

Celebrate every time you make a shift, have a new awareness or insight, make a new choice, take an action in
alignment with what you desire or experience a miracle.
Celebrations can be as simple as pausing to acknowledge
a shift with a deep breath and a smile, a dance of joy,
a hoot and a holler, sharing your success with a loved
one or anything else that feels fun and acknowledges the
shifts and miracles taking place, whether small or huge.

8

For Men: Easy Strategies that Work with Women

And . . . You'll Be Pleasantly Surprised by the Results!

SO HERE'S THE SHOCKING NEWS. IF BOTH YOU AND YOUR partner have grown up in a culture with little, if any, healthy relationship mentoring, chances are she doesn't know how to let you know what she wants in a way that really works for both of you—at least not any more than you know how to provide it and vice versa. This chapter addresses some of the common types of challenges that cause men to feel confused or frustrated with women, followed by some easy strategies that work with women, even if they're not yet aware of it.

A handful of relationship challenges I've heard from men:

Challenge #1: We are discussing dinner. My partner is frustrated and can't specify what she wants—only what she doesn't want. What do I do? I want to be part of the solution not part of the problem.

Challenge #2: How do I get more sex?

Challenge #3: How can I avoid giving up the things that are important to me (some that don't include her) without hurting her feelings?

Challenge #4: How can I tell my partner something she doesn't want to hear without getting a big reaction?

Easy strategies that work well with women

Strategy #1: Remember to acknowledge her experience and feelings first. Let her know you're on her side.

To use this in response to Challenge #1, (expressing what she doesn't want but not what she wants): Open your heart and acknowledge her frustration. Say something like: "I hear your frustration and I'm here, ready to support you in whatever way I can." This phrase can be adjusted as needed to offer your sensitivity and support in many situations. You have just made a huge shift to being "part of the solution not part of the problem." Apply this strategy in combination with Strategy #3. For

Challenge #2, how to get more sex: You might find your partner much more receptive to sex when she's already feeling connected, supported, loved and adored. When you are attentive to her experience and acknowledge her feelings, you are showing her your love and connecting with her in a real and meaningful way.

This strategy applies to Challenges #3 (not giving up your important things) and #4 (telling something your partner doesn't want to hear), too! Combine this with Strategy #3 (great questions to ask) to make it even more potent. You won't need to control or change her feelings if you learn how to hold space for her to move through them. You might think of her feelings as waves coming through. One after another they swell and subside. Flowing *with* them works better than resisting them, and the truth is that you really don't have control over them anyway, so it is best to simply become a good surfer.

Don't discuss anything that requires a decision, or anything important or sensitive, on an empty stomach.

Strategy #2: Don't discuss anything that requires a decision, or anything important or sensitive, on an empty stomach.

My Love and I discovered this strategy many years ago when we noticed that we had a tendency to have arguments before dinner. We made a commitment to save all sensitive or important discussions and decision making for after eating and also when we were feeling well rested. From that point on, we did not attempt to discuss issues or create solutions to problems when we were either overly tired or needing to eat. This shifted things instantly for us and allowed us to realize how well we were able to navigate our issues and challenges together when we gave ourselves more optimal conditions for co-creating solutions. I invite you to experiment with this even if you think low blood sugar has no influence on you. Note: Along these lines, I have also noticed that when one or both partners have had a good dose of caffeine and/or sugar (including alcohol), this can create more tense or volatile conditions that are not ideal for navigating sensitive or challenging issues. Again, keep this in mind if your discussions are escalating in nonproductive ways.

Applying this strategy to Challenge #1 (your partner's inability to express what she wants): It is important to understand that before dinner, especially if either she or both of you are already feeling hungry, it is likely that you have low blood sugar, which is not the ideal time for extended discussions of any kind. If at home, this would be a good time for a quick appetizer to give you both more breathing room and patience. Also, if your partner usually needs to eat more frequently than you, she is probably at the blood sugar level where decisions are nearly impossible. She will be more stable if you get her to have some dinner sooner rather than later. You can be part of the solution by making your best suggestion based on what you know she likes and whatever will expedite dinner. If there are no big objections, then move forward with this plan.

Strategy #3: Build yourself a toolbox full of great questions. Use them often.

Let go of judging or fixing your partner, just be curious. Choose and adjust questions to make them appropriate for your partner and the situation. Follow the energy. You might choose just a few that you feel comfortable with to start. Being open and cultivating an attitude of curiosity with your Love creates the kind of closeness most women want. Asking questions with a real desire to know more about her will let her know you're interested in her, that you care about her, that she's important to you, that you respect her enough to ask rather than assuming you already know . . . and so much more. And when you are asking the questions, you also have an opportunity to focus the conversation in directions of interest to *you*.

Here are some sample questions and inquiry ideas for your toolbox to get you started. I've proposed a bunch of ideas for each of three scenarios: checking in, gathering more clarity and offering support. Just ask one question at a time. Depending on the situation and her responses, you might start with a check-in question and follow up by gathering more clarity or offering support. Choose a few questions that fit for you and modify them to your own style and situation.

Check in:
On a scale of 1-10, 10 being off the charts amazing, how was your day/event/meeting? What was the most inspiring/fun/edgy/empowering moment or highlight of your day? How are you feeling? You look radiant/sad/upset/mischievous. What's up? What's happening for you right now?

Gather more clarity:
How so? Tell me more about that. How do you feel about that? What about that is important to you? What else about that is important to you? What was the gift/blessing in that? What was fun/inspiring/meaningful about that? What about that are you really wanting me to hear/understand? Can you simplify that for me? Or (with a sense of humor) can you simplify that into male speak?

Find out how to best support her when she's upset:
How can I support you most in this moment? How can I hold space for you? Would a hug help? Do you want to be held? Do you need me to do or take care of something so you can take some time for yourself? How can I assist you in this? Or I'm here for you and I'm not sure how to be the best support for you right now. Please guide me. Or simply be a listening presence . . . and you might say, "I'm with you." or, "I'm listening." or, "I feel you."

This strategy could contribute to Challenge #2 (getting more sex). Sharing emotional intimacy and connectedness can be potent aphrodisiacs. So your toolbox of questions may surprise and delight you by enhancing your sexual intimacy as well.

Strategy #4: Learn your partner's preferences. Some women are very tuned into their preferences and only need to be asked and/or heard when they share them. Some women have not yet given themselves permission to have preferences, much less express them. Until they give themselves permission to acknowledge and have preferences, the preferences may come out sideways. And you can help by noticing and honoring her preferences even when she hasn't done so.

It can be incredibly powerful to study and know your partner's preferences. It is an act of caring when you know and honor her preferences. This expression of caring is endearing for many women, allowing them to feel truly loved and adored. For special surprises, learn her preferred treats. It may be flowers, chocolate or a spa treatment. If you study well, you'll even know if she has a favorite chocolate, flower or masseuse. Surprises don't have to be big, even a thoughtful card or a little note can be special. So start doing your research and enjoy the responses you receive from your pleasantly surprised partner.

Use this act of caring in combination with Strategy #1 (acknowledging her) for Challenge #2 (getting more sex). You might find that your Love is much more interested in sharing sensual love and intimacy when she's already feeling the sense of intimacy you're cultivating by being sensitive to her feelings, experiences and favorite things.

If she struggles with knowing and honoring her own preferences, you may even go to the point of keeping a journal of what works and what doesn't work so you can surprise and support your partner in identifying her preferences and honoring them. If you do this gently and respectfully, it can be very healing for her.

Knowing your partner's preferences may also come in handy in moving towards a solution for Challenge #1 (unable to express what she wants), because you can probably offer up some choices of eateries that would likely get an affirmative response. And, if she's too hungry to choose, and you already know her favorites, then you can just go for it without hesitation.

Strategy #5: Give advice only when asked.

Women will ask you for advice when they desire it. You can let your own example be the model that inspires her. Women usually care more about how you show up than how cleverly you speak. Maybe you've heard the old adage, "actions speak louder than words." You will gain more respect by respecting your Love than by giving her suggestions and advice before she asks, especially if the suggestions and advice are not in alignment with her own goals or desires. When she does ask for your advice, she is much more likely to trust you and therefore you will have the most potent impact if you first use Strategy #3 (questions to gather more clarity) and Strategy #4 (knowing her preferences). Ask

> *We need to be able to both skillfully speak our truth and to hear or receive another's truth.*

some great questions to find out what kind of advice will support her in moving toward her highest vision.

Here's an example:
Your partner wants to buy a car and she asks you what kind of car you think will be best for her. You could start by asking how she plans to use the new car. Will it be for commuting or for road trips? Or what? What are the most important features of a car to her? You can assist her by listing some things to consider. Now, I'm not an expert on cars so you may be able to think of even more appropriate questions to ask her. The point is that when you honor her agenda by asking questions with curiosity and respect before *you offer any advice, your advice will be valued exponentially. Oh, and this kind of thoughtful advice giving can be very sexy, too.*

Strategy #6: Speak your whole truth.

If speaking your truth is a new strategy for you, I promise that this will create a lot more ease and make a huge difference in your relationship. When truth is restored, it often brings back love, trust and sexual intimacy as well. Even when our words lie, in my experience, our bodies don't. How is your body expressing what you haven't been speaking?

You may have learned to stop telling your truth by a gradual process of osmosis, by example or by painful experiences in your past. If you are like most of us, you probably haven't received much guidance or mentoring in this essential relationship skill, either. What I often see with couples is a pattern of one person who lies or withholds information while the other is likely to react when told the truth. I work to resolve this from both ends. We need to be able to both skillfully speak our truth and to hear or receive another's truth. Doing so with grace, takes this skill to the level of artistic mastery. And an ungraceful truth spoken is better than the damage of withholding. Speaking your truth takes courage, practice and commitment. Start with the commitment, gather your courage and any guidance or support you need, and begin practicing.

In order to speak your truth to others, you first have to tell the truth to yourself. So start by asking yourself some questions. What am I afraid of, here? What am I wanting right now? What is the desire underneath that? How can I give myself what I truly desire? Usually we don't tell the truth because we have a belief that we have to manipulate in order to get what we want. So, how's that working for you? What if there's a much simpler, easier way to get what you want?

Your truth is about you, your feelings, desires, values, choices and actions. Practice speaking your clear and simple truth. Do your best to leave out any added judgments, conclusions or interpretations. Learning to know the difference will add more grace to your communications and, at the same time, minimize reactions. Your partner is most likely to react to judgments, conclusions and interpretations. So, if you simply share what's true, you might be pleasantly surprised by shifts in the quality and ease of your communications. This will help with Challenge #4 (telling her what she doesn't want to hear). Combine this truth-speaking strategy with Strategy #1 (acknowledging her feelings) to be super effective in navigating Challenges #3 and #4. Remember, don't try to control her feelings, just surf with them.

For Challenge #3, look honestly at your own priorities and be clear with your Love. Don't set yourself up by giving up what is important to you or by being misleading because you think it will go over better. Those are old manipulative tactics that don't really work to get what you want. And, your priorities may be changing if you are making room for a new relationship. Give yourself space to explore what will be in alignment with your current values. The key is to get in touch with the balance that truly works for you and share the truth with your partner as you do. It can be a dance to find the perfect balance of "together" and "apart" in your relationship. Dance with it and stay honest.

Strategy #7: Honor your freedom and hers. Take responsibility for your choices.

When we come together in a place of honoring each other's freedom and choices, we open up possibilities to thrive together in co-creativity. When you honor and take responsibility for your choices, it becomes easier to collaborate and make plans and you can drop the need for any manipulation, excuses or apologies. When you invite and allow your Love to do the same, then your relationship becomes clean and clear. You know that when you are together it is because you are both choosing it.

Here's a sample of what this might look like:
"My desires for this weekend include some time in the garden, yoga on Sunday morning and some unscheduled time with you. I'd also like to meet up with the guys at some point to plan our May camping trip. What would you like to do with me? And what else is important for you this weekend?"

This strategy goes hand in hand with Strategy #6 (speak your whole truth) to address Challenge #3 (not giving up important things). Be who you are and allow yourself to evolve. If you hesitate to express what is truly important to you, you might also look at what you are afraid of losing. Here are some questions to get clear within yourself: "What is my fear, here? Am I willing to honor my Love's freedom to choose what's best for her? If I am willing to let go of my fear and choose for myself, what would my ideal balanced life look like?" When you are clear, honest and confident in what you desire, it makes it easier for her to choose what's right for her. When you're both clear and honest, everyone can relax and enjoy living freely.

Questions to ask:

Asking questions opens us to new possibilities and solutions. No need to know or find the answers. Let the answers come to you. Just ask the question with a sense of curiosity, speaking out loud if possible, and then release it. An answer may come instantly or later. It may come in thoughts, words or as guidance in another form. Be open and stay tuned. Asking opens the door to miracles.

How can I tune into what's most important to me in this moment and align myself with it?

What if I am totally honest?

What if I tell my whole truth in my relationships?

What can I share with my partner that I've been withholding about what I'm afraid of?

What can I share with my partner that I've been withholding about what I truly desire?

What expression of freedom do I value most and how can I honor that myself?

How can I be more honoring of my Love's freedom to choose what's best for her?

What is my ideal balanced life and how can I align myself with it?

Tools and practices to use:

1) The 7 Easy Strategies—this is the list without the explanations for easy reference

Strategy #1: Remember to acknowledge her experience and feelings first. Let her know you're on her side.

Strategy #2: Don't discuss anything that requires a decision, or anything important or sensitive, on an empty stomach.

Strategy #3: Build yourself a toolbox full of great questions. Use them often.

Strategy #4: Learn your partner's preferences.

Strategy #5: Give advice only when asked.

Strategy #6: Speak your whole truth.

Strategy #7: Honor your freedom and hers. Take responsibility for your choices.

Actions to choose:

This is simply a list of actions based on this chapter that you might choose to take on your proactive path. I offer them as options to support you in bringing the material from this manual to life. You may choose one or more from this list or you may find something else from the chapter that inspires your action. The practices work miracles when practiced! And to enjoy the shifts and miracles, you'll need to take actions!

continued...

Actions to choose continued

Action 1: Choose one of the 7 strategies from this chapter to apply in your daily life. Choose one that stands out for you as a solution to an issue that arises in your relationship. Once you practice, explore and integrate that first one, then you might add another one and so on.

Action 2: Empower your Love in her own evolution by sharing this book with her. Invite her to read it with you and if it feels fun you might choose some practices together.

Bonus action: Write to me with your love miracles and I will celebrate each and every one! You will also be contributing to our love evolution movement by creating an expanding culture of healthy, thriving relationships in the world. I am exhilarated and motivated by your love miracle stories and the extraordinary results that unfold when you implement these simple yet powerful practices into your life.

Celebrations!

Celebrate every time you make a shift, have a new awareness or insight, make a new choice, take an action in alignment with what you desire or experience a miracle. Celebrations can be as simple as pausing to acknowledge a shift with a deep breath and a smile, a dance of joy, a hoot and a holler, sharing your success with a loved one or anything else that feels fun and acknowledges the shifts and miracles taking place, whether small or huge.

9

Co-Creating Solutions Without Sacrifice or Compromise

A Radical Approach to Conflict that Brings You Together in Collaboration.

HAVE YOU EVER HAD A CONFLICT WITH A LOVED ONE THAT you couldn't resolve? And you either argued about it all the time or you avoided dealing with it because you knew someone would have to compromise and you didn't want it to be you? Or you felt so certain there was no way to resolve the conflict peacefully that you were afraid to bring it up?

Well, you are not alone. Almost all of our common models for resolving conflicts, especially in our most intimate relationships, include compromise or sacrifice. In fact, we are taught that if we really love someone we would be willing to sacrifice for them. Sometimes we even use sacrificing ourselves regularly as a way to show our love. And most times, it is because this is what was modeled for us by our parents or other significant role models as we were growing up. If your parents modeled this for you, I have to ask you: were they happy? And how much fun was it for you to live with parents who sacrificed their well-being or happiness? What I've noticed about this sacrificial way of loving is that it creates a certain level of suffering and misery, not to mention resentment, for one or both partners, which affects the health, happiness and well-being of the whole family or household.

So, I'm delighted to share with you now that it's possible to turn conflicts into solutions without sacrifice or compromise. Here is my Co-Creative Solutions Process—my most powerful process for shifting opponents in conflict into collaborators with solutions. This Co-Creative Solutions Process works miracles with both couples and groups to resolve core issues at the level of root cause. To give you an idea of how well the process works, here are a few comments I've heard from people after they have gone through this process together:

"We all witnessed a miracle that day. Our hearts were filled with love and gratitude and deep appreciation for each other . . . It was powerful!"

"The world could use as much of this type of conflict resolution as it can get."

"Everyone comes out a winner!"

The concept is simple. However, the skills require practice and experience, so please be patient with yourself and each other as you cultivate these skills. As human beings, we are incredibly resourceful problem solvers when given all the parameters of the problem. Therefore, the trick in applying our resourcefulness to our interpersonal problems is to first gather all the parameters without letting our fears and limiting beliefs get in the way.

The more you honor, respect and are receptive to each other, the more this creates an environment in which it is easy to speak your truth.

In this chapter, I will give you a detailed, step-by-step description of the process, so you can begin practicing with it. Give yourself quite a few practice runs on lighter issues to allow you to get a better feeling for how it works before you use it with a more intense conflict. I also offer additional support for this process in my couples work and in the form of trainings. Witnessing others going through the Co-creative Solutions Process, or being guided through it yourself, makes it much easier to learn and apply on your own.

Co-creative Solutions Process

Step One: Creating a safe container with specific agreements and a commitment.

It is important to get a "Yes" from each person for every agreement before moving forward. Without these agreements and a commitment in place, this process is unlikely to yield desirable results. It would be like pouring all of your precious water supply into a container with holes. So create the safe and solid container before you start pouring yourself into the rest of the process. Once you have a clear "Yes" from each person, move to the next agreement.

Agreement #1
Start by making a commitment to coming up with a solution that meets the essential desires of all involved and letting go of any attachment you have to your picture of the solution. Are you willing to commit to co-creating a solution that honors your individual and collective desires and that works for all involved?

Agreement #2
Nobody gets to be wrong. This includes you. Do you agree to nobody being wrong?

Agreement #3
The more you honor, respect and are receptive to each other, the more this creates an environment in which it is easy to speak your truth, which greatly enhances the flow and efficiency of this process. Do you agree to be honoring, respectful and receptive to all values, desires, preferences, needs and feelings?

Agreement #4
All feelings are valid and welcome and belong to the one feeling them. As human beings, we move through different feeling states naturally and no one else gets to argue with how we feel or take the blame for how we feel. Do you agree to welcome all feelings in this process and own your own feelings?

Agreement #5
Everyone gets a chance to speak their truth without interruption. Speakers pause every 2-5 sentences to allow the listener(s) to

ask clarifying questions. Do you agree to take turns speaking? And when you are the speaker, to speak what's true for you and pause often enough to allow the listener(s) to follow and understand what you are sharing?

Agreement #6
Listen from your heart with loving kindness and curiosity to excavate the mysterious and unknown values, desires, preferences, needs and feelings that will allow you to create a satisfying, and even delightful, solution for the highest good of all. Do you agree to listen with curiosity and kindness in an effort to uncover the hidden details needed to create the most satisfying and fun solution?

Agreement #7
We treat each other respectfully and honor each person's right to choose. We each make our own choices. Nobody else is responsible for our choices. Do you agree to choose for yourself and to respectfully honor each other's choices?

Step Two: Centering

Take a moment to breathe and connect with your self. Sit up tall, with your shoulders relaxed back, to open your heart with love and acceptance toward yourself and each other. Tune into how you are feeling physically, emotionally and energetically, without judgment or needing to change anything. Then tune into what you are wanting from this Co-creative Solutions Process. How do you desire to be or to show up in this process? What is your intention for yourself as you do this process? After several breaths of tuning in to what arises, share your intentions with each other. Respond to each intention with a simple "thank you."

Step Three: Choosing and reviewing your roles.

Decide who will be the first speaker and the other person will be the first listener. (When this is done for a group process, everyone else is a listener and only one person facilitates by asking questions.) The listener will ask the questions. Listener, your role is to listen from your heart with loving kindness and curiosity to become clear on the known and to excavate the mysterious and unknown values, desires, preferences, needs and feelings of the speaker that will allow you to create a satisfying and even delightful solution for the highest good of all. Speaker, your role is to answer the questions by expressing what's true for you with ownership (this means taking full responsibility for your own feelings, desires and choices) and pausing every 2-5 sentences to allow the listener to ask clarifying questions.

Notes: Decide who will take notes. Everyone will be jointly responsible for remembering to make these notes even though only one of you may actually be writing the notes. (In a group process, a third person would take notes while checking the accuracy with group members along the way.) I like to track the key details: 1) Succinct summary of each person's essential desires, and then the collective ultimate outcome or higher purpose you are seeking to create with this solution; 2) each person's needs, preferences, values and desires, concisely expressed, to be considered as you co-create the solution; and 3) the Ultimate Solution you co-create, with all agreements included. The first two are mostly to use as reference during your process together. The third is essential. It is the outcome of your process, your ultimate co-created solution and all the agreements within that Ultimate Solution. You'll need to be clear that you agree on what's written so it's easy for you to follow through on the agreements. Aim for simple clarity using as few words as possible.

Step Four: Getting clear on the positive outcome desired.

Listener, please ask: "What is the positive outcome or essential desire you are seeking to fulfill with this solution?" Speaker, please respond with a succinct summary of the positive outcome you desire. Then pause. Listener, from a place of curiosity and loving kindness, please ask any clarifying questions to get to the essence of the core outcomes the speaker desires. Speaker, please allow yourself to be curious about yourself and what's most important or essential to you. Listen within and dig deeper if needed.

Note to the Listener/facilitator: Use clarifying questions to focus on and uncover the essential desire or core value that the Ultimate Solution will need to fulfill in order to work for the speaker. Follow your inner curiosity and intuition.

Examples of clarifying questions:
Is there anything else we need to know about that?
And what will that give you?
How will that make a difference for you?
How will that benefit you?
And what will that do for you?
What essential desire is at the root of that?
What core value will that nourish for you?

Switch roles and repeat steps three and four.

Step Five: Co-creating your Ultimate Solution

Review the summary of the all the essential desires and the collective ultimate outcome or higher purpose you seek to fulfill in co-creating this solution. Now, take a few breaths and tap into your

What is the most delightful, possible solution we can create to fulfill our collective essential desires and higher purpose?

most creative solution-oriented self to make a list together of all the possible solutions in answer to these questions: "What is the most delightful, possible solution we can create to fulfill our collective essential desires and higher purpose? List everything that comes to you even if it seems whacky. What else is possible? List everything else that comes to you. Now, each pick your top three choices based on the following criteria: the ones that feel right to you, that meet all the essential desires in your summary and that seem likely to create the most delightful solution for all involved. At this point, it may already be incredibly obvious to you both which solution will work best. If so, follow that and clarify the details. If that hasn't become crystal clear yet, then explore the solutions you picked in common. If none are common, share what it is about each of your top choices that stands out for you and then choose one of each other's top three to explore further. What highlighted qualities could you add to improve these solutions even more? Or how might you combine them in a way that would be more delightful for all involved? What else is possible?

Step Six: Celebrating and recording your Ultimate Solution!

Yay! You did it! Congratulations! When you reach your ultimate co-creative solution, take a few moments to celebrate in a fun way. You might take a few deep breaths and some sighs or expressions of joy, or shared hugs, or some dancing or appreciations or expressed gratitude. Then write your Ultimate Solution clearly with all the agreements included. Be as specific as possible and indicate times for follow-up actions.

Questions to ask:

Asking questions opens us to new possibilities and solutions. No need to know or find the answers. Let the answers come to you. Just ask the question with a sense of curiosity, speaking out loud if possible, and then release it. An answer may come instantly or later. It may come in thoughts, words or as guidance in another form. Be open and stay tuned. Asking opens the door to miracles.

How can I be even more tuned in, helpful and aware as a collaborator?

How can I be even more aware of the unlimited possibilities available to us?

Is there anything else we need to know for this to be easy and graceful?

What will make the most difference in creating the highest possible solution?

How can we align with the divine to create the best possible solution for all?

What essential desire is at the root of what we each want?

What core values are we collectively seeking to nourish in our Ultimate Solution?

What is the most delightful, possible solution we can create to fulfill our collective essential desires, values and higher purpose?

What qualities could improve our solution or be even more delightful for all involved?

What else is possible here?

Tools and practices to use:

1) Forgiveness Practice:

(Note: If you have resentment or blame, I highly recommend doing this practice regularly and at least once before you begin the Co-Creative Solutions Process, especially if you are doing it on your own.)

Always start your forgiveness practice by forgiving yourself first. Here's the format:

I, (your name), forgive myself for any way I have hurt myself, or (name of a person you are choosing to forgive) or anyone else.

Say the forgiveness vow slowly, out loud, with heart-felt intentions. Say it at least 3 times or until you feel a shift. Next, move your attention to another person you wish to forgive and follow this format:

I, (your name), forgive (name of a person you are choosing to forgive) for any way she/he has hurt me, or herself/himself or anyone else.

Again, say it out loud, 3 times or until you feel a shift, speaking slowly and with intent to forgive and release.

Then move on to the next person who comes to mind. Continue until no one else comes to mind and you feel complete.

The beauty of these specific forgiveness scripts is that they address the unconscious aspects of blame, including that we are probably blaming or shaming ourselves internally and that when we hurt someone else, we are almost always hurting ourselves as well. In this way we also acknowledge that the same is likely to be true for the one we need to forgive.

Do this forgiveness practice every day, ideally morning and evening before bed, and whenever you feel yourself holding a grudge of anger, resentment or blame toward anyone, including yourself.

This is a life-long practice. Stay with this daily forgiveness ritual until you no longer find yourself blaming anyone for anything and you feel empty of resentments. Then you can take a break from the practice until the next time you experience blame or resentment, and simply bring back the daily ritual.

Forgiveness and gratitude are my two most powerful practices for restoring inner peace, and opening up the free flow of love and joy. I find, now, that after doing the forgiveness practice for a few days, I am free of blame and grudges for a while. Then whenever a new or old one arises, I start the practice again until I feel clear and free once more. My clients have also reported profound shifts and wonderful feelings of joy and lightness from this practice.

Please also note: Forgiveness has nothing to do with condoning unacceptable or abusive behavior. We can forgive and simultaneously maintain clear, healthy boundaries.

continued...

Tools and practices to use *continued*

2) Courageous Communication Practice:

Begin by connecting with yourself. Take a few deep breaths and notice how you feel physically, emotionally and energetically. Check in and notice what's true for you in this moment. Ask yourself if there's something you are wanting right now. If so, acknowledge it to yourself. Practice noticing and then sharing what you notice with your partner. Is there anything you're hiding or withholding from your partner? If you feel afraid to share, that's a good place to begin. You can simply say, "I feel scared to tell you . . . I'm afraid (name what your fear is)". Sometimes it helps to have a list of feelings to help identify and put words to what you are feeling. You can find one online compiled by the Center for Nonviolent Communication. This list can also help make the distinction between feelings and thoughts, which are not usually as valuable for creating connection and can even get in the way of closeness. Learning what thoughts to share and how to share them in a way that deepens connection and builds trust is a more advanced practice so start with your physical and emotional feelings. Next, you can practice sharing your desires and making clear requests.

3) Deep Listening Practice:
Practice listening with all your senses. Listen deeply, beyond the words. Practice listening without reacting, interrupting or taking anything personally. Remember to breathe as you listen. Cultivate an attitude of curiosity. Ask about feelings or desires to invite deeper connection like an archeologist digging to unearth the treasures. Ask questions rather than assuming you understand. You'll learn more about the unique ways your partner experiences the world that way. And your partner will experience the sweet gift of feeling heard. As you listen to your partner, do your best to stay connected with yourself too.

Actions to choose:

This is simply a list of actions based on this chapter that you might choose to take on your proactive path. I offer them as options to support you in bringing the material from this manual to life. You may choose one or more from this list or you may find something else from the chapter that inspires your action. The practices work miracles when practiced! And to enjoy the shifts and miracles, you'll need to take actions!

Action 1: Review the sections and practices from chapter 2 regarding opening the Gates of Love with the Keys of Courageous Communication and Deep Listening. The practices, which I have also included in the "Tools and practices to use" section for this chapter, will help prepare you with the skills to succeed in your Co-creative Solutions Process.

continued...

Actions to choose continued

Action 2: Review chapter 3 thoroughly. Everything in that chapter sets the foundation for your success in this Co-creative Solutions Process.

Action 3: Find a qualified friend, mediator or coach to help facilitate this Co-creative Solutions Process for you.

Action 4: Choose just a few questions to ask from the lists at the end of this or another chapter to write on sticky notes and post them in places where you'll see them often. Choose questions that inspire you to make shifts in the direction of the new choices and outcomes you desire. Each time you see one of your posted questions, pause and ask it out loud if possible, or silently if necessary. Remember to breathe and allow the question to resonate for a moment. Keep asking and stay open for guidance and miracles to come.

Bonus action: Write to me with your love miracles and I will celebrate each and every one! You will also be contributing to our love evolution movement by creating an expanding culture of healthy, thriving relationships in the world. I am exhilarated and motivated by your love miracle stories and the extraordinary results that unfold when you implement these simple yet powerful practices into your life.

Celebrations!

Celebrate every time you make a shift, have a new awareness or insight, make a new choice, take an action in alignment with what you desire or experience a miracle. Celebrations can be as simple as pausing to acknowledge a shift with a deep breath and a smile, a dance of joy, a hoot and a holler, sharing your success with a loved one or anything else that feels fun and acknowledges the shifts and miracles taking place, whether small or huge.

10

Savoring Dessert

Sweet and Tasty Morsels
to Enhance Sexual Intimacy

INTIMACY IS BOTH BLISSFUL AND ESSENTIAL IN DEEP AND lasting love. Sexual intimacy is one way we express, celebrate and expand our intimate love connection with each other. Emotional intimacy, honesty, trust and vulnerability open the gates to sexual intimacy as a fully alive and joyful expression of the wholly embracing love we share. Our intimacy is a gift worth savoring.

This chapter offers just a small taste of the sweetness and richness you can cultivate in your sexual intimacy together. In my experience with couples, I have found sexual intimacy to be so deeply personal and so often in need of healing that I feel it is best explored with the safety and support of live coaching. Sexual trauma and mis-information is so prevalent in our culture that most of us have been sexually wounded and misguided, often unintentionally, and we may not even be aware of our own sexual trauma. Our wounds and challenges offer us opportunities to tap into our resourcefulness, deepen our understanding and expand our capacity for an ever-richer experience of love and aliveness.

My intention here is to inspire your appetite for what else is possible in the realms of sexual intimacy. First, I'll share my own story of sexual healing to highlight our human resilience and potential for turning our wounds into our blessings. Then we'll explore, expand and reframe how we view sexual zest, foreplay and sex.

Transforming sexual trauma to sexual intimacy

At sixteen, I began an intimate relationship that gave me the safety of patient, adoring love, which helped me to heal from childhood sexual trauma and abuse. My boyfriend (teenage name for my Love) showed up for me with love, respect and curiosity. He expressed his desire to know me by asking questions, deep questions and playful questions. I felt fully seen, heard, felt and adored by him. Our relationship was founded in friendship, open honesty and trust.

We shared many kinds of experiences together. We met working on a lighting crew for community theatre and continued to do that regularly together. We went on bicycle rides and hikes, went swimming and to the movies. We spent hours in "turned on" states sharing intimately in playful, open, honest conversations as well as kisses and cuddles, often without any other sexual stimulation. He was a young man of eighteen at the time, with plenty of sexual vitality and a sincere desire to please me, yet any attempts he made to give me further pleasure would often trigger flashbacks of my sexual abuse followed by an emotional release. The level of patience he showed me was a gift that I received as true love. He received my openness and honored my boundaries in a way that allowed me to discover what I now call *sensual love play*.

In the safety of this playfulness, sensitivity and ever-deepening closeness, I was able to expand my ability to receive and share pleasure that, in turn, continued to deepen our intimate connection. This exploration and discovery continued over the next twelve years, and during that time we were able to share a beautiful, loving journey of growth and evolution together, while also expanding and discovering our capacity for sexual intimacy. In healing myself from sexual trauma, I was able to truly get in touch with what felt fun, loving and yummy to me. I was absolutely clear that I prefer to be seen, treated and appreciated more like one appreciates a flower or a tree—beautiful to my core or essence, rather than as a sex object. I am forever grateful for this relationship, which has evolved into a deeply loving, commitment of friendship for life. Our mutual commitment and the open, embracing quality of our relationship supported me on a path of turning my sexual abuse and trauma into a catalyst for uncovering what else is possible in the realms of love and intimacy. From my own healing journey, I now offer you a few of the insights and reframes that helped me. May these insights inspire awareness on your journey of deepening your capacity for real love and intimacy.

Opening your flow of aliveness

You could think of your sexual zest as the life force flowing through you. If you are alive, then the pulse of that sexual vitality is still flowing, at least to some degree. In our culture, we are so afraid to be with our sexual vibrancy that we cut off or damp down this potent source of creativity, motivation and aliveness. In order to shut down our sexual zest we also disconnect from our bodies, our breath and our sensual experience of life, and then we wonder why we feel so tired and our bodies are complaining. What if we embrace our sexual vibrancy and aliveness? What if we learn how to feel it, be with and enjoy our sexual zest? What if the choices we make and the actions we take with our sexual zest is really up to each of us?

I invite you to open up to your own sexual vitality. Let yourself feel it flowing through you. I know how sexual passion can seem intense, uncontrollable and even scary at times. When your zest feels beyond control, take a few deep breaths. Breathe into the passion you feel and just be with it. You don't need to resist, use or release your zest and vitality. For now, learn to be with this energy that naturally flows through you. Let yourself feel and listen to your body. Let yourself breathe, stretch and move your body. Notice what happens. You might begin to notice how simply allowing your sexual zest to flow brings you more aliveness, creativity and vitality. You might discover that you have more motivation than you realized.

Reframing sexual intimacy with an appetite for play

If you've read my story of sexual healing earlier in this chapter, you might have noticed that my healing journey began with an extraordinarily long-lasting phase of foreplay. Being abused by my stepfather, starting when I was nine, introduced me to sex as serious, forceful and painful. Later, sharing that long-lasting phase of foreplay with my boyfriend felt safe, playful and healing to me. It also allowed me to tap into, discover and express more of me. I was truly blessed with an experience that inspired me to reframe foreplay as a safe way to begin exploring, healing, learning, discovering and opening up new possibilities together.

Discover how simply allowing your sexual zest to flow brings you more aliveness, creativity and vitality.

In my reframing, foreplay can include all the ways you keep the sexual connection alive between you and your Love. All of your daily interactions can be foreplay. Foreplay itself may not always be explicitly sexual, though it can still be exceptionally sexy—building a foundation of shared moments, experiences, connection, trust and appreciation. What creates delectable foreplay is savoring being together whether in a sweet kiss or in collaborating on a garden project. I will tell you that, for me, working on a project side by side with my capable, care-full, respectful man is *incredibly sexy* foreplay. Foreplay can go on for hours or days, leading you in and out of sex, bringing this appetite for play into your sensual love play.

As children, we played without an agenda or focus on outcome, and this is a quality we can create in our sensual love play to enhance our bonding and fun together. Let yourself explore and play together with all your senses alive. Be curious about your Love. Ask playful questions and deep questions, creating safety and sharing vulnerability. Explore and play to find out what is pleasurable, getting to know your Love's preferences and favorite flavors while learning your own. Allow yourself to receive the love expressed in the level of sensitivity you share in these moments of being together. Follow the energy you co-create, wherever it leads, embracing the ebb and flow, unfolding in waves of heating up and cooling down, into a deeper recognition of each other.

Sensual love play does not require intercourse, or even orgasms, and it could include either or both. It is more about being physically, sensually and emotionally present together, sharing pleasure and vulnerability and deepening connection in an open, honoring exploration of the many flavors of intimacy from tender to fiery. This will nourish your emotional intimacy, which is essential to vibrant sexual intimacy, as well as being one of the foundations for thriving relationships. Whatever your play includes, it is likely to be worth savoring.

A delicious evolution to slow lovin'

I have found that when the focus is on connecting in plea-sure and play instead of on achieving orgasms, then waves of pleasurable sensations often come readily, effortlessly and nat-urally. These natural, whole body orgasms have an enlivening quality, way beyond just a physical release. In fact, when you stay sensitively tuned in to yourself and each other, following inclinations to pause or shift to soothing and softening instead of stimulating, this can inspire wave after wave of expansive orgasmic euphoria. Our bodies always tell the truth, so sensual love play reveals us to ourselves and to each other.

Allow your sensual love play to unfold into discovery together with all your senses alive, touching, listening, sharing, looking into each other's eyes, smelling, and tasting. It's also important to have the sensitivity to realize when you've checked out, or when you've gone into autopilot. Checking out is really an invitation to tune in more deeply with each other, since it usually signals that something is bubbling up to be revealed. We usually check out when we are afraid to feel or share something. This is a time to offer each other patience and kindness, loving encouragement and curiosity.

Creating a sweet and delicious experience means just showing up for the adventure together in our innocence and openness. We have come to realize that slow food is more fulfilling, enjoyable, and enriching. In a similar evolution, we can realize the intimacy-enhancing potential of slow lovin'. So slow down, and savor the moment with your partner. Allow yourself to see and be seen, to breath and feel together in the ever expanding embrace of love.

How fully present can you be with each other: physically, emotionally, and spiritually?

How completely naked and vulnerable can you be together?

Healing ourselves and our culture from sexual disconnection

Sex and intimacy are vastly misunderstood in our culture. To foster intimacy, a closeness that allows us to touch and be touched within our whole being, requires us to remove more than just our clothes. As a culture, we often treat sex as if it is an itch that needs to be scratched, by building up sexual, erotic tension just to relieve it. This approach becomes more about stimulating body parts and less about cultivating real intimacy and hugely contributes to a growing sense of emotional and sexual disconnection. In truth, it leads to emptiness, loneliness and cravings rather than a sense of being filled and nourished by the love we share.

Our culture is simultaneously sexually suppressed and obsessed. On one hand we are programmed to ignore and hide our sexual feelings rather than enjoying the vitality that naturally flows through us. On the other hand sexy images and the promise of sex are constantly used to sell everything from toothpaste to cars to soda. So we buy and consume rather than actually feeling what we feel, physically, spiritually or emotionally.

The way I see it is that whenever we don't allow ourselves to feel what we feel or acknowledge what's really present, it comes out sideways—expressing itself in unhealthy or indirect ways. I see the use of pornography as a sideways expression or symptom of our sexual disconnection. The availability and consumption of pornography have become pervasive in our culture, furthering emotional disconnection and sexual obsession while deepening the underlying feelings of loneliness, isolation and shame that we are attempting to soothe with it. Our longing for real love and intimacy cannot be fulfilled on this path, which is one of many ways we have learned to avoid and distract ourselves from unresolved pain and wounding, and fears that we are unloved and unlovable. The use of pornography allows us to create a fantasy that the sex object of our attention is or

Creating the fully embracing love and sexual intimacy you desire starts with a choice to show up courageously and honestly.

would be enjoying, appreciating and pleasuring us into the ultimate orgasm, which on some level we imagine to be an expression of the love, acceptance and worthiness we long for. Sadly, all of this vanishes once the fantasy is over and we are hooked into recreating it again and again.

Unfortunately, the use of porn can keep us from sharing real intimacy, even with a loving partner and relationship. One who frequently uses porn as a substitute for real closeness may struggle to shift from focusing on a sex object and fantasy to being sensitively present for making love with their partner. The crazy thing is that it doesn't even come close to the euphoric bliss we have the capacity to share in exquisitely sensuous union with our beloved.

The good news is that truly intimate and blissful sex with your partner is still within reach. Healing these patterns of sexual disconnection begins with awareness followed by a new choice. This chapter is only meant to open up your awareness of what else is possible—you may require much more support and expert facilitation. As with emotional intimacy, the deep closeness and sexual intimacy we long for is a choice, not a given, in sexual relationships and marriage. Creating the fully embracing love and sexual intimacy you desire starts with a choice to show up courageously and honestly. Bring a sense of curiosity and playfulness to your exploring and unfolding together. Start by cultivating new awareness and consciously choosing to shift from habitual fantasy toward cultivating the honesty, presence and vulnerability needed for real connection. Then you can open yourself to discover the depth of truth, beauty, pleasure and closeness you are able to share with your Love.

Questions to ask:

Asking questions opens us to new possibilities and solutions. No need to know or find the answers. Let the answers come to you. Just ask the question with a sense of curiosity, speaking out loud if possible, and then release it. An answer may come instantly or later. It may come in thoughts, words or as guidance in another form. Be open and stay tuned. Asking opens the door to miracles.

What if I embrace my sexual vibrancy and aliveness?

What if I allow myself to feel, be with and enjoy my sexual zest?

What if the choices I make and the actions I take with my sexual zest are really up to me?

How fully present can I choose to be with myself and my Love—physically, emotionally, and spiritually?

What would it take to create a safe haven for us to share more intimately?

How truly naked and vulnerable can I allow myself to be?

How can I be show up even more sensitively, courageously and honestly with my Love?

Tools and practices to use:

1) Opening to Aliveness Practice:

I invite you to open up to your own sexual vitality. Let yourself feel it flowing through you. I know how sexual passion can seem intense, uncontrollable and even scary at times. When your zest feels beyond control, take a few deep breaths. Breathe into the passion you feel and just be with it. You don't need to resist, use or release your zest and vitality. For now, learn to be with this energy that naturally flows through you. Let yourself feel and listen to your body. Let yourself breathe, stretch and move your body. Notice what happens. You might begin to notice how simply allowing your sexual zest to flow brings you more aliveness, creativity and vitality. You might discover that you have more motivation than you realized.

2) Slow Lovin' Practice:

Slow down and savor your sensual love play together. Allow your love play to unfold into discovery with all your senses alive, touching, listening, sharing, looking into each other's eyes, smelling, and tasting. Awaken the sensitivity to realize when you've checked out, or when you've gone into autopilot. Checking out can be an invitation to tune in more deeply with each other, since it usually signals that something is bubbling up to be revealed. We usually check out when we are afraid to feel or share something. So offer patience and kindness, loving encouragement and curiosity at this time.

Savor each moment. Allow yourself to see and be seen, to breath and feel together in the ever expanding embrace of love.

Actions to choose:

This is simply a list of actions based on this chapter that you might choose to take on your proactive path. I offer them as options to support you in bringing the material from this manual to life. You may choose one or more from this list or you may find something else from the chapter that inspires your action. The practices work miracles when practiced! And to enjoy the shifts and miracles, you'll need to take actions!

Action 1: Give attention to honoring the transition from sensual love play to whatever is next, whether it is going to sleep or moving into the rest of your day. Take a few moments to hold each other or breathe together. To allow even a brief time for integration will bless you with a graceful transition and will allow the euphoric quality of your love play to linger with you.

Action 2: Find some inspiration by watching children co-creating their play together. Notice how they explore, connect, choose and collaborate together. Take this into your sensual love play.

Action 3: Express your creativity and find a new way to bring more play into your intimate connecting and sharing.

Action 4: Tell the truth. Share something with your partner that you've been afraid to share. Open the doors and the windows. Bring the truth into your relationship. It will free you both if you've been withholding anything from each other. Review Strategy #6 in Chapter 8 if you need more support in taking this action.

Bonus action: Write to me with your love miracles and I will celebrate each and every one! You will also be contributing to our love evolution movement by creating an expanding culture of healthy, thriving relationships in the world. I am exhilarated and motivated by your love miracle stories and the extraordinary results that unfold when you implement these simple yet powerful practices into your life.

Celebrations!

Celebrate every time you make a shift, have a new awareness or insight, make a new choice, take an action in alignment with what you desire or experience a miracle. Celebrations can be as simple as pausing to acknowledge a shift with a deep breath and a smile, a dance of joy, a hoot and a holler, sharing your success with a loved one or anything else that feels fun and acknowledges the shifts and miracles taking place, whether small or huge.

11

Postscript

HAVING READ AND PRACTICED YOUR WAY THROUGH this manual, you've already covered a lot of ground on your rich and rewarding journey to discovering what else is possible in love, marriage and intimacy.

Let's celebrate your conscious, courageous steps by taking a look at how far you've come.

After acknowledging your deep longing for real love and closeness, and exploring the importance of love to your health and well-being, you began your proactive path where most fairy tales and movies end: bringing awareness to your day-to-day, moment-by-moment choices.

You received your own set of keys to the gates of love with access to essential relationship tools and practices you weren't taught in school—the essential relationship tools and practices that work to cultivate sustainable love, trust, fun and intimacy.

Then you were able to examine the habits that create distance in your relationship and practice ways to turn them around. You also learned about becoming collaborators and creating a safe haven together, and then considered the three steps for mending, soothing and learning from your mis-takes. Hopefully you've been putting the tools and practices to use and are well on your way to awakening the deeply nourishing love and intimacy you are meant to share.

Maybe you've even expanded the flow of love in your life by nourishing and replenishing yourself. Have you experimented with the 6 CHARMS to being deliciously adored, yet? What about the 7 practical and easy strategies to address some of those little challenges that sometimes trigger big fights in your intimate relationship?

And . . . you *now know* it *is* possible to turn your conflicts into solutions without sacrificing or compromising. Right? You even have the step-by-step guide to take you through the process.

Last, but not least, we opened up the extraordinary potential of sexual intimacy worth savoring.

What would happen if you continued to integrate the tools and practices in this book, instead of setting it aside as a book you have finished reading? Could it radically enhance your relationships or even save a marriage?

If you've begun applying even one new practice so far, you are taking steps on your proactive path to your very own happily ever after. Stay with it. Exploring, playing, discovering and then celebrating each and every step, big or small, along the way!

Love is a practice. And we get to choose it, prioritize it and commit to it—again and again.

Since you've made it this far, I know you have already made the choice to show up in love—conscious, courageous and committed— and you've made this choice more than once. My heartfelt wish for you is that this is radically improving your relationships, creating the life and love you truly desire. The changes you've made are rippling out, touching all those whose lives you touch, expanding the capacity for real love and harmony in the world. I invite you to spread this evolution of love by sharing this manual and these practices with your dear ones, with your family and friends, with everyone you know . . . so our children can grow up with the relationship guidance and role models that were missing for many of us.

What else is possible now?

The Four Radical Commitments for joyful living, loving & thriving

If you've been applying the tools and practices you've learned in this manual to your day-to-day moments, you may be ready to take your relationship to a new level with the Four Radical Commitments, that integrate all of what you've already been practicing.

"Radical" means "of or relating to the root of something." These core commitments are the roots that nourish and stabilize your relationship so that it grows and thrives through many seasons.

Radical Commitment #1: Collaboration

This commitment is about being on the same team through the high roads and the rough bumps instead of competing, resisting and warring with each other. It's a commitment to co-creating solutions that work for both of you without compromising or sacrificing.

It's also an opportunity to invite and inspire the highest in each other, showing up more fully in love and in life, expressing your spirit, following your calling. Imagine feeling fully seen, embraced and adored by your partner, who holds your vision with you—and the buoyancy that provides as you expand into your fullest expression, touching this world in the way that only you can.

Here's the commitment to share with your partner:

"I commit to collaborating with you."

Radical Commitment #2: Discovery

This commitment is about bringing lightness to your human adventures together, recognizing that it's truly a grand experiment. We are evolving. Our relationship is evolving. Our life, our relationship is a work in progress. Being open to discovery means setting aside your assumptions, judgments, stories and conclusions. Instead you can enjoy the new unfolding of yourself, your partner and your relationship each day. This will keep your relationship fresh and fun through every season.

Here's the commitment to share with your partner:

"I commit to bringing a sense of playful curiosity, humor and discovery to you, me and us."

We are evolving. Our relationship is evolving. Our life, our relationship is a work in progress.

Radical Commitment #3: Full Disclosure

This commitment is about 100% honesty and ownership. This is the most radical commitment both in the sense that it is so essential and that it is radically opposed to what most of us have learned by osmosis from our family and culture.

Here's the commitment to share with your partner:

"I commit to telling the whole truth about what I feel, desire and do."

Radical Commitment #4: Safe Haven

This is about allowing yourself and your partner to be exactly who you are with all your strengths, charms, brilliance, flaws, shortcomings, imperfections, uniqueness and similarities, power and vulnerability. It means honoring both of your preferences, your callings, your yes's and your no's, your freedom and your choices. This is a commitment of choosing to show up with love, kindness, understanding and tenderness instead of criticism and judgments of good or bad, right or wrong, fair or unfair.

Enjoy the new unfolding of yourself, your partner and your relationship each day.

When you create this safe space within yourself and with your partner, your interactions will naturally evolve into an expression of respect. The old habits of disrespect, such as condescending tones, lecturing, ranting, raging or criticizing will naturally dissipate as you rely on the tools, practices and love wisdom you have available to you to navigate the issues and challenges in your relationship as opportunities to grow closer.

Here's the commitment to share with your partner:

"I commit to being and creating a safe haven for me and you."

Where we're headed...

Together we are now awakening deeply nourishing love and intimacy in our own relationships, inspiring a cultural shift that will allow succeeding generations of children to grow up held, embraced and mentored in healthy, happy, loving relationships. I feel a passionate calling to touch and transform enough relationships with this deeply nourishing love and intimacy that our children grow up knowing how to create close, thriving relationships of their own.

If you, too, hold this vision in your heart, please join me in fulfilling my mission.

A love evolution has begun. It needs to grow and expand exponentially to make a real difference for our children, in our culture and toward a peaceful world. We are the love catalysts the world needs. Together we can spread this love evolution movement far and wide. The time is Now! Let's surf this wave together into a future of love for all of us.

Let's do this for ourselves, for our children and for our world!

May your relationships embrace and nourish you. May you adore and be deliciously adored, always.

In love,

Tracie

*A love evolution has begun.
It needs to grow and expand
exponentially to make a real
difference for our children, in our
culture and toward a peaceful
world. We are the love
catalysts the
world needs.*

Celebrations!

Write to me with your love miracles and I will celebrate each and every one! I am exhilarated and motivated by your love miracle stories and the extraordinary results that unfold when you implement these simple yet powerful practices into your life. Together we are creating an expanding culture of healthy, thriving relationships in the world.

Tracie Sage
The Love Catalyst Coaching Institute
PO Box 390
Williams, OR 97544

http://www.traciesage.com/
your-celebrations-and-love-miracles/

541-479-5128

Lightning Source UK Ltd.
Milton Keynes UK
UKHW02f0915250918
329483UK00014B/1820/P